NANYANG PERSPECTIVE

The Publications Committee of the Asian Studies
Program will consider all manuscripts for inclusion
in the series, but primary consideration will be
given to the research results of graduate students
and faculty at the University of Hawaii. The
series includes monographs, occasional papers,
translations with commentaries, and research aids.

Orders for back issues and future issues
should be directed to The University Press of
Hawaii, 535 Ward Avenue, Honolulu, Hawaii 96814,
USA. Present standing orders will continue to
be filled without special notification.

Asian Studies at Hawaii, No. 13

NANYANG PERSPECTIVE

CHINESE STUDENTS IN MULTIRACIAL SINGAPORE

Andrew W. Lind

Asian Studies Program
University of Hawaii

The University Press of Hawaii
1974

Library of Congress Catalog Card Number 74-75816

ISBN 0-8248-0330-2

Copyright © 1974 by The University Press of Hawaii

Manufactured in the United States of America

CONTENTS

LIST OF TABLES

PREFACE

Nearly five years have elapsed since the eruption of the riots in Malaysia on May 13, 1969, and time alone undoubtedly has done much to quiet the racial tensions engendered throughout Southeast Asia by those unfortunate disturbances. Relationships among the several racial groups in nearby Singapore were inevitably exacerbated by that conflagration, and at that time even the most objective reporting of what was transpiring could be regarded in some circles as a further threat to the peace and welfare of the community.

It was to be expected, therefore, that a sociological study conducted among students in one of the two major universities in Singapore just four months after the riots would bear some marks of that traumatic experience. There was reason to believe, however, that a clearer and more incisive analysis of race relations in the region might be derived from informants who were fully conscious of what happens in such recurring crises than from persons who lacked such vivid experience.

Delaying publication for nearly five years places the study in a historical as well as a sociological perspective, and this should also assist in reducing somewhat the fears that examination of such trying encounters might simply serve to reopen old wounds. Apprehensions were indicated by knowledgeable readers of this book as recently as early 1973 that some of the quoted statements by Nanyang University students, if they were made public, might "cause /sic/ racial antagonism in these parts" or at least might be exploited by "elements on both sides of the Johore Strait, who are ever ready to foment racial strife and sour relations between the two governments." Whatever practical considerations may once have existed for placing constraints on the publication of an objective report on the reactions of university students to the world in which they live seem now, however, to be overshadowed by the greater importance of providing the general public with a realistic account of what it means to be participants in such a community atmosphere.

Although the developing economic ties of the countries of Southeast Asia with the rest of the world had injected into these regions much the same sort of dilemmas of racial and ethnic relations with which an industrialized nation like the United States had been compelled to grapple considerably earlier, there had been relatively little disposition to recognize even the existence of similar

x

problems in Asia and Africa. It had been widely assumed that most of the difficulties associated with the presence of diverse ethnic groups in these areas were a consequence of the domination by European powers and that these difficulties would largely disappear with the withdrawal of the Western colonialists.

Unfortunately both social scientists and the indigenous administrators who have displaced the former political overlords have preferred not to probe too deeply into questions of potential inter-ethnic tensions, on the theory that it is better to "let sleeping dogs lie." As a result, systematic studies of Southeast Asian race relations in the postcolonial period are almost nonexistent. Surely the time has come for realistic analyses, by social scientists, of such extremely critical aspects of community life as those involved in ethnic and racial relations, and it is hoped that this peripheral approach by an outsider may induce scholars better qualified by extensive first-hand acquaintance in Southeast Asia to attack such studies more directly.

Andrew W. Lind
Emeritus Senior Professor
of Sociology
Honolulu, Hawaii, 1974

INTRODUCTION

A university whose student body consists only of
a single racial group would seem at first sight
a distinctly unpromising locale for a study of race
relations. When, however, that university is located on the island of Singapore, and the students
are drawn from communities as racially and culturally diverse as those of Southeast Asia, the pic-
ture changes quite completely. Nanyang University,
as its name implies, was conceived and has remained
since its founding an institution for overseas
Chinese, in which the Chinese language has been the
chief medium of instruction. Yet the two thousand
students enrolled there in 1969, although born and
raised primarily within a transplanted Chinese
environment, had all associated to a greater or
lesser degree with Malays and Indians and usually
with the other peoples of the region, including
Indonesians, Eurasians, and Europeans, toward all
of whom they had inevitably derived some impressions, either favorable or unfavorable.

For a visiting American sociologist, with a
long professional interest in the field of race
relations, the temptation to explore so potentially
rich a source of hidden knowledge was too great to
resist, even within the limited time and available

resources. A joint invitation from the East-West Center at the University of Hawaii and from Nanyang University in Singapore to spend nine months at the latter institution to assist in the establishment of a teaching and research program in sociology, with special reference to race relations, seemed to offer an excellent opportunity to initiate some research in a promising but hitherto neglected field.

The outbreak on 13 May 1969, of a series of bloody race riots in neighboring Malaysia, involving relatives and close acquaintances of many of the university students and occupying the central place in the news of the entire population in Singapore for many weeks thereafter, seemed to call for special attention to issues of race relations as affecting the morale on the Nanyang campus during the latter half of that year. By October 1969, the emotional distress growing out of the Malaysian holocaust had sufficiently subsided so that the Chinese students of Nanyang could view their associations with the various peoples of Southeast Asia with some degree of objectivity and calm. The recollections of the tragic experiences just a few months earlier were still sufficiently vivid in the minds of all Nanyang students, however, to color considerably their racial sensibilities by

xiv

the time such a study could be undertaken.

Because of its location outside the city of Singapore--fifteen miles from the city center-- it soon became apparent that if research were to be combined with teaching and administrative consul- tation, the university itself was the best locale for all these activities. Additionally, the fact that the university administration had indicated an interest in securing a frank expression from the students of their reactions to certain aspects of university life--something that had never been attempted before on any extensive and systematic scale--offered further justification for focusing major attention on the campus.

As a means of combining the more immediate and practical concerns of the university adminis- tration with the more remote and theoretical in- terests of the visiting sociologist, plans were formulated to submit to all students of the univer- sity a twelve-page questionnaire at the time of registration for the second semester early in October 1969. With the assistance of faculty colleagues and students in the social sciences, an instrument, covering 130 different specific ques- tions and calling for both objective and open- ended answers, was finally evolved, and arrangements were made through the Deputy Vice-Chancellor and the Department Chairmen for the distribution of the questionnaire to each of the students. Quite understandably, the response of both faculty and students to such a venture, which inevitably must have seemed to some as an intrusion on their time and privacy, varied quite considerably from one department to another.

Perhaps the most striking aspect of the experiment was the generally high degree of participation in a wholly voluntary extracurricular activity, for which neither students nor faculty would derive any particular credit but from which hopefully the university itself might gain some benefit. The slightly more than two-thirds of the students who were willing to devote the thought and the time required to complete the questionnaire--no less than an hour and extending far beyond that minimum for those who wrote at greater length--was much larger than the regular Chinese members of the faculty had thought possible on the basis of previous experience. This generous response from the Nanyang students reflects not only a willingness to adhere to administrative expectations, but more specifically reflects a positive desire to unburden themselves of sentiments regarding the university and community for which there previously had been little opportunity.

xvi

Cooperation in completing the forms was requested in the opening sentences, "as a means of arriving at a better understanding of the students of Nanyang University and of the communities from which they come . . . . Although it is hoped that the findings from this study will enable the University to serve the students and the community better, the research is being conducted independently of the University by a visiting social scientist." The students were further urged to express themselves "as honestly, thoughtfully, and . . . as freely and unreservedly as possible, knowing that no one will know how you answer any of the questions." They were expressly instructed not to add their names at any point, and no record was kept of those who did or did not return their completed forms. For the benefit of the larger proportion of the students whose command of English was limited, a Chinese version of the questionnaire was available and their answers to the open-ended questions could also be in Chinese. This, of course, necessitated subsequent translation into English of the answers to such questions for the benefit of the American sociologist and the readers of this book.

The subject matter of the questionnaire covered four major areas of student experience--

their personal background, their family and community background, their campus experience, and their outlook on life in Southeast Asia. The first two dealt with basic information essential for an understanding of the nature of the student body as a whole, while the third provided data of special value to the administration, and the fourth was designed to answer questions on racial and community issues with which I was primarily concerned. A report based primarily on the responses to the twenty-two questions relating to student experience on the Nanyang campus, covering such areas as housing, medical care, food, counseling, library facilities, and other matters of strictly internal administration, was submitted early in 1970 for use by the faculty and administrative officers, and these findings enter only incidentally in the present study.

Any serious effort to understand the meaning of reactions to such an impersonalized instrument as a questionnaire, however, requires a good deal more than merely statistical summaries of the data which it directly provides. To place the responses of the students in any proper perspective, it was obviously necessary to take account of the historical setting of the wider community from which the Nanyang students have emerged. Similarly, it is

xviii

only against the background of the seemingly endless flow of immigrants from China and the peculiar
economic and social forces to which they were subjected in Southeast Asia that such a unique institution as Nanyang University and its distinctive
selection of students can be comprehended.

Thus the relatively circumscribed venture in
cooperative research of a group of college students
develops into a project requiring some presentation
of the background of the movement of the Chinese into Southeast Asia, their economic and social ad-
justments there, and the circumstances leading up
to the founding and growth of an unprecedented and
unparalleled institution of higher learning. It
was discovered, however, that although there was a
reasonable body of literature on the expansion of
the Chinese into Southeast Asia, especially with
reference to its economic impact, relatively little
attention had been directed to the problems resulting from the Chinese interaction with the
people of other racial and ethnic backgrounds re-
siding within the region.

The first two chapters of this book are devoted to a summary of Singapore's history as affecting the immigration and interaction of the
various racial and ethnic groups and more especially
of the Chinese.

The third chapter provides a brief review of the circumstances leading to the establishment of this unique institution of higher learning, some of the difficulties encountered during the first decade of its existence, and some account of the manner in which this Chinese university has evolved in its multiracial environment during the late 1960s.

The concluding three chapters draw chiefly, although certainly not exclusively, upon the experience of the Nanyang students as reflected in their responses to the 1969 questionnaire. Chapter 4, entitled "Personal Resources for a Multiracial Society," seeks to depict the common and distinctive qualities of the Nanyang students, including those of character and personal goals and objectives.

Chapter 5 focuses directly upon the racial and ethnic perspectives of the students, with special reference to their exclusiveness on the one hand and the evidences of racial tolerance on the other hand. Utilizing a simple "social-distance scale," all twenty-one of the racial and ethnic groups likely to have entered into the experience of the Nanyang students were rated in terms of their acceptability as marriage mates, and a composite score was derived for each. More of the depth and flavor of the student reactions appear, however, in the written interpretations through which they

xx

sought to explain or justify their individual ratings, and without them the statistical ratings would have been much less meaningful.

The final chapter, entitled simply "Nanyang Perspectives," brings together findings relating to the student interests in national and world affairs, with special reference to such issues as communalism versus multiracialism, racial equality, and individual freedom.

Since this book was conceived as possibly having a fairly broad reading public, concerned with contemporary developments in Southeast Asia, less attention has been given to the methodological refinements or the technical terminology than some readers might expect from a professional sociologist; but for these lapses, if such they be, I make no special apologies. Had it been possible for me to do so, I would have preferred to devote more than the nine months available at Nanyang in order to enlarge the range of my friends and acquaintances with both faculty and students and to deepen further my associations with them. It would also have been advantageous to have had additional time to probe into the experience of the alumni and former students of Nanyang, of whose achievements and general experience I have unfortunately so little tangible knowledge.

The present study has, of course, been largely exploratory in nature and is also subject to the limitations inherent in any research by an outsider with restricted time and resources. It could, however, serve a useful purpose in calling public attention to this largely neglected but increasingly critical area of human relations in Southeast Asia. One could hope that social scientists from the region itself, with their long familiarity with the languages and customs and their natural entrée to life among the people, would probe more deeply into the complexities of intergroup relations. Certainly Nanyang University constitutes a natural locale and laboratory for more detailed and refined studies of the role of the Chinese in the changing Southeast Asian scene, just as other institutions of higher learning offer similar opportunities and obligations for research on other aspects.

It would be impossible to list the names of all the persons to whom I am indebted for assistance, many of whom, especially among the students at Nanyang, are quite unknown. These unnamed students, however--1,303 of them who participated in the survey--individually and collectively contributed the greater part of the information upon which this study is based, and I wish to express

xxii

my sincere appreciation for the part they have played. It is possible to single out a few members of the Nanyang administrative staff and faculty who were especially helpful in launching and in seeing this study through to completion. Dr. Victor Fic, Professor and Chairman of the Department of Government and Public Administration, was most directly and helpfully involved in both the initial planning and in the execution of the study among the Nanyang student body, contributing generously not only of his own intimate knowledge of the university and of the region, but also of the facilities of the Institute of Southeast Asia, of which he was also the director. Both the Vice-Chancellor, Professor Rayson Lisung Huang, and the Deputy Vice-Chancellor, Lu Yaw, gave most generous support to the project, and colleagues on the faculty, notably Professors Sung Ming-Suen, Raymond Liew Pak Choong, and Ong Teck Hong, made helpful suggestions in drawing up the questionnaire. Professor Tan Soei Tien and members of his staff in the computing center made possible the transfer of the statistical data to punch cards and their summarization in the tables around which much of the discussion in chapters 4, 5, and 6 is organized. Unquestionably the one person who carried the heaviest burden in almost every aspect of the study, except the actual preparation of the final report, was my graduate assistant, Chuah Toh Chai--translator, interpreter, consultant, organizer of student helpers, liaison with faculty, and general factotum--to him I am especially grateful.

Finally, I wish to express appreciation to the East-West Center of the University of Hawaii, to Nanyang University, and to the Asia Foundation for their combined administrative and financial support, which made possible this entire venture. An extension of my original grant from the Institute of Advanced Projects of the East-West Center enabled me to continue during 1970 with the analysis of the research data and the preparation of this book.

THE CHANGING IMMIGRANT WORLD OF SINGAPORE

Singapore has been called many different things--
haven for pirates, a great commercial emporium, eye
of the Malaysian needle, pearl of Southeast Asia,
and many more--but all the many terms have commonly
carried some implication of a center for trade. It
is in that context of a marketplace for the exchange
of goods, people, services, and ideas that Singapore
must be conceived of for this study. Here in micro-
cosm are revealed the stresses and strains among
the varied peoples of a large portion of the modern
world, and for an understanding of the sort of
leadership likely to emerge in that region, some
attention must be given at the outset to the total
setting within which the university students of
today live and move.

A Peninsular Island

Geographically, Singapore represents the tiniest
speck of land within a vast region of possibly a
tenth of the world's surface. Obviously its restricted land area of 224.5 square miles has not
been the magnet to attract numerous and varied
activities and people from outside its borders.
Visitors to Singapore for the first time still

marvel that an island so small and so lacking in natural resources could house, much less support, a population of over two million people.

Situated less than a hundred miles from the equator, it might be assumed that the island's torrid climate would deter settlement by any large number of people. Actually, of course, the climatic conditions on the island are far more favorable to human life and comfort than many inland areas much more distant from the equator. Although both temperatures and humidity remain fairly high throughout the year--ranging from a daily minimum average temperature of 73 degrees Fahrenheit to a maximum of 89 degrees and a daily minimum average humidity of 70 percent--these are far less debilitating than in most other parts of Southeast Asia or even in many parts of the so-called temperate regions. Being a relatively small island and thus refreshed at all times by the cooling winds from off the sea, Singapore is not only bearable climatically, but is to many people a distinctly pleasant place in which to live.

Physically, Singapore is rather unprepossessing. The low-lying terrain, of which only 10 percent is more than 100 feet above sea level and reaching a maximum elevation of 581 feet, presented in its native state a somewhat typical tropical

2

landscape, with numerous short streams or rivers
and the accompanying mangrove swamps. Although the
island was almost entirely covered with vegetation
in 1819 and contained a rich variety of tropical
flora and fauna, it was almost wholly devoid of
mineral resources, except for the clay, granite,
and sand essential for building and construction
purposes.

Although much of the land was suitable for
agricultural use, it has never been devoted exclusively to sustain the residents of the island, and
even if all the tracts adapted to such cultivation
had been so employed, they could not have provided
a livelihood for the half million to two million
people who have lived there during the past fifty
years. This is not to minimize the part that
agriculture has played and continues to play in the
economic support of Singapore's population, but even
during the nineteenth century when agriculture had
reached its highest percentage strength as a source
of income for the island, it was chiefly in terms
of plantation crops, such as nutmeg, pepper, gam-
bier, coconuts, and rubber, which were valued for
export to a world market, and not produce for local
consumption. Within the postwar period the proportion of economically active males engaged in all
forms of agriculture in Singapore had dropped to

6.7 percent in 1947 and still further to 3.3 percent in 1966.

Commerce and trade have been, of course, the major economic force attracting hundreds of thousands of persons into this restricted land area and which has colored their style of life ever since. But it is this tiny island's geographic position, so strategically situated with reference to the whole Southeast Asian quarter of the world, which has given to Singapore its dominant strength as a trading and commercial center. The search for a center from which the East India Company, reenforced by its military power, might dominate the trade of this vast region, was the major consideration leading to the founding of Singapore as a British port in 1819.

Stamford Raffles' recognition of this unimpressive parcel of land at the extreme southern tip of the Malay peninsula--part of the peninsula surely, but also separated from it by a narrow body of water--for its tremendous commercial potential undoubtedly constitutes a principal basis of his rightful claim to distinction. He saw in Singapore not merely the forbidding mangrove swamps which harbored innumerable pirates but the "excellent anchorage and small harbours . . . . peculiarly adapted for our object . . . conven-

4

ient and commanding . . . for our China trade
passing down the Straits of Malacca, and every
native vessel that sails through the Straits of
Rhio must pass in sight of it," and he expected
the island to become "a great commercial emporium
and a fulcrum whence we may extend our influence
politically as circumstances may hereafter require."[1]

The commonly accepted claim, attributed first
to Sir Richard Winstedt, that "the history of
Singapore is written mainly in statistics,"[2] has
reference, of course, chiefly to the phenomenal
expansion of trade and human population, primarily
from the environing regions of Southeast Asia.
Within five years of its founding, Singapore had
developed commercial contacts, valued at S$4,451,000
with such widely scattered areas as the Malay
peninsula, the Philippines, Java, Sumatra, Celebes,
Borneo, and Bali.[3] This was a consequence, not
only of Singapore's fortunate location with reference to the entire world of Southeast Asia, but
perhaps as much of the wise policy of free trade
initiated by Raffles and continued by both the
East India Company and the British Colonial Office
after it assumed control in 1867. Between 1823 and
1864 the trade of the colony rose from £2,563,124
to £13,252,175 and its entrepôt services included

not only the East Indies and Malaya, but also
Siam, Cochin China, China, and the countries of
Western Europe.[4] The expansion of Singapore's
commerce with the rest of the world has been equally
spectacular in point of volume during the twentieth
century, such that by 1967 it was the fourth
largest port in the world, based on the tonnage
of ships entering the harbor. This was in large
part a function of the city's emergence during the
first half of the century as the world's top
trading center for tin and rubber and the major
port of export of these commodities for Malaya.

The ties of economic and political interdependence with Malaya have always been matters of
special concern to Singapore, if only because of
the close physical proximity to this neighbor with
such vastly greater possessions of land, physical
resources, and population. In a sense, Singapore
has always been only a minor appendage on the Malay
Peninsula, but by virtue of its strategic location
with reference to trade and its separate existence
as an island, there have always been grounds for a
separate identity and a different approach to the
problems of the individual and society. As a
commercial center and entrepôt, Singapore's outlook
has necessarily been cosmopolitan and adaptive in
its free and open contacts with an ever expanding

6

world, whereas the hinterlands and primary producing areas, such as Malaya, Indonesia, and other peasant-populated regions of Southeast Asia, are more inwardly oriented to the problems of preserving their resources and their traditional values.

The Dynamics of Trade

By virtue of its development as a trading metropolis, Singapore has come to exercise the sort of influence over its hinterland, most notably the Malay peninsula, which the marketplace always exerts over the areas which utilize its facilities. Despite its theoretical nature as an equalitarian and impersonal type of relationship which both parties are free either to accept or reject according to their own self-interests, trade over an extended period of time may nevertheless appear to be contributing more to one side than to the other. It would be difficult to imagine that the exchange of goods and services in Singapore could persist and grow over the past century and a half except as a relationship thought to be mutually advantageous to the participating parties and regions.

At the same time, however, trade is a stimulating and exciting sort of experience which inevitably attracts to the marketplace people of diverse backgrounds and capabilities. Singapore, no less than other cities "along the Main Street of the World," has been able to recruit persons with specialized skills and services on the basis of the greater freedom of movement and opportunity it could offer as compared with any of the more settled agricultural communities. As a consequence, in part of the concentration in the metropolis of so many and varied abilities and the facilities for gaining additional knowledge, Singapore has also succeeded in bargaining more effectively in the exchange of its resources with the other areas in Southeast Asia. Thus, it has become increasingly apparent that in the course of what was supposedly an equalitarian exchange of goods and services, Singapore as a whole has fared considerably better than the primary producing areas that have supplied the commodities for the metropolitan market.

Although probably less than a third of the whole population of Southeast Asia is now engaged in subsistence farming, in all areas except Singapore well over half, and frequently over 80 percent of the population, in the region is engaged in some form of agriculture,[5] in which the level of income is commonly low. Accurate objective data comparing the level of income in the countries of Southeast Asia unfortunately are not available, but statistics provided by the United Nations indicate that Singapore's per capita gross national product was, in

8

the late 1960s, well over twice that of any other
country in Southeast Asia, and except for East and
West Malaysia, it ranged from four to ten times
that of all these countries.[6]

Some of the more striking aspects of the manner
and extent to which Singapore has become oriented
to a modern commercialized economy are summarized
in a highly informative statement by a prominent
geographer on the occasion of the city's 150th
anniversary.[7] It indicates that Singapore, as
the smallest state in the region, is the most densely populated, with almost 9,000 persons per square
mile, but its people nevertheless enjoy the
region's "highest standards of living." These
standards or ideals, as distinguished from those
elsewhere in Southeast Asia, are "almost wholly
oriented toward objectives similar to those found
in Western industralized countries, namely, the
acquisition of material wealth and the production
of goods and services beyond basic subsistence
needs. . . . individual initiative and the entre-
preneurial spirit are dominant." While recognizing
Singapore's strategic location at "one of the major
maritime crossroads of the world" as its greatest
economic asset throughout the past century and a
half, attention is also called to the "nonnatural"
resources acquired from its colonial past in the

form of "commercial, financial and credit institutions, the trading associations, the stable currency," which play so important a part in today's
trend toward industrialization.

Political stability during both the colonial
and postcolonial periods of course has been a major
prerequisite for the economic growth of the island.
The phenomenal increase in population from less than
two hundred persons in 1819 to more than two
million a century and a half later could not have
occurred without guarantees of civil order and the
protection of life and property. Neither would
Singapore have been able to attract its widely
reputed reservoir of "experienced, strongly motivated and industrious people" without some assurance
of law and order within the community, no matter
how great the economic inducements might be.

Singapore's outstanding success as an industrial and commercial stronghold of the modern world,
greatly exceeding that of any neighboring centers
in Southeast Asia, has not been achieved without
certain social costs, particularly in terms of the
stresses and strains on the peoples of diverse cultural traditions drawn together there. Most of the
remaining portions of this book are devoted to
the exploration of this somewhat neglected area
of Singapore's experience, as it appears to affect

10

the lives of a significant element of the island's
largest racial group.

Sorting and Settling the People

Every community organized around a marketplace
attracts not only goods from abroad but also the
people to engage in the buying and selling, and in
this respect Singapore is no exception. While the
bulk of the commodities involved in Singapore's
entrepôt trade is drawn from the neighboring re-
gions--rubber, tin, and timber from Malaysia;
pepper from Sarawak; oil from Sarawak and Brunei;
rice from Thailand--the majority of the people have
been recruited in successive stages from more remote
areas, chiefly from South China and South India.
Even the minority of Malays in Singapore's population during the first third of the present century
had come in large part--not from the Federation of
Malaya--but from overseas areas, notably Indonesia.

Although it is accurate to say that most of
the residents of the centers of trade and commerce
around the world are either immigrants or the
descendants of immigrants who had come there to buy
or sell goods or services, it must also be recognized that their movement may have been initiated by
quite other considerations. The people who have
come to Singapore from other areas over the past
150 years were, in large part, peasants whose cir-

11

cumstances of life in their native villages of China, India, or Indonesia had become so difficult as a result of overpopulation or some natural catastrophe that they were virtually forced to seek their livelihood elsewhere. Other factors too, such as geographic contiguity to the outside world, political disaffection, and possibly special cultural emphases upon enterprise and adventure, may have contributed to the especially large flow of migrants from certain districts, including the Fukien and Kwantung provinces of South China.[8] Probably the vast majority, however, were seeking to escape from intolerable conditions at home, and they hoped that somewhere overseas they might find a better place in which to live.

Although the first of the immigrants to Singapore, following its founding in 1819 by Stamford Raffles, were chiefly Malays and Chinese from Malacca who were attracted by the excitement and greater opportunities of the British free port, the major flow soon began to originate in the over-burdened peasant communities of South China. Singapore's immediate and phenomenal preeminence as a trading center for Southeast Asia had almost as direct an impact upon the growth in numbers and the selection of its population. Raffles himself claimed that within four months of its founding

12

Singapore had "received an accession of population exceeding 5,000--principally Chinese, and their number is daily increasing,"[9] but more guarded estimates indicate that of a total population of 10,683 in 1823, the Chinese immigrants constituted 3,317 or 31.0 percent. Estimates of population continued to vary considerably throughout the first half century of the city's existence, but the available data indicate that during the first 21 years the number of inhabitants had increased to approximately 35,000, of whom one-half were of Chinese birth or origin and slightly less than one-tenth were immigrants from India.

Throughout the period of nearly fifty years that Singapore continued under the jurisdiction of the East India Company, the mounting number of immigrants from overseas areas could be largely absorbed as ordinary workmen in the trading activities of the port or as laborers on the agricultural enterprises on the island or nearby Johore, and a sizable number were able to establish themselves as independent tradesmen. During this period in particular, the Chinese immigrants were overwhelmingly adult males, estimated in 1860 to have been 15 men to every woman, and consequently their segregated communities in the trading center or in the rural areas of the island were characterized by the common social abnormalities,[10] which emerge wherever extremely high sex disproportions prevail.

The demand for labor in the developing mines and plantations of Southeast Asia, especially from the last quarter of the nineteenth century onward, offered one of the most promising outlets for the refugees from the overcrowded peasant communities of the adjacent regions. The nature of these institutional forerunners of capitalistic enterprise on the frontier is that their need for a substantial number of steady workers cannot be supplied by the sparse resident population, and it is therefore necessary to import them from densely populated regions with a surplus of able-bodied men seeking employment. The presence of large deposits of tin and the discovery of the possible industrial uses of rubber, together with the tremendous expansion of the world markets for these two commodities, encouraged both European and Chinese entrepreneurs to undertake vast mining and plantation enterprises in Malaya. Singapore became one of the major ports through which the flow of indentured labor from China and India was distributed to these operations in Malaya and other parts of Southeast Asia and to which many returned after they had completed the terms of their contracts.

As early as 1871 the Chinese alone constituted

14

a moderately large city of nearly 35,000 persons or
56.2 percent of all the residents of Singapore,
while the Indians added another 10,754 or 11.9 percent of the total population. A sizeable, although
unknown proportion of the Chinese were, of course,
the children or descendants-further-removed of
the original overseas immigrants and sometimes
were of mixed Malayan ancestry, but the size and
concentration of the immigrant community was such
as to retain, for both the immigrants and their
offspring in this Southeast Asian community, the
language and much of the culture of the homeland.
Even at this early date, Singapore had already
become predominantly a Chinese city, through which
there was "a constant and direct flow of migrants
backwards and forwards . . . . a centre of the distribution of Chinese labour throughout the British
and Dutch territories,"[11] and of which it could also
be said that "the Chinese immigrants lived their own
life according to their own ways. And . . . even
if it had been decided that they should acclimatize
themselves culturally and socially, there was no
'national' pattern of living to which to conform."[12]

The striking growth in size of Singapore's
population from less than 100,000 persons in 1871
to over 418,000 just 50 years later did not alter
substantially the character of the city as consist-

15

ing predominantly of transient male immigrants, with the attributes that one would expect in such an abnormally constituted community. The Chinese character of the city became even more accentuated, rising from slightly over half in 1871 to three-quarters (75.2 percent) of the entire population in 1921. The very high disproportion of males to fe-males in 1871 of 6.17 to 1 among the Chinese and of 4.49 to 1 among the Indians had declined to 2.13 to 1 among the Chinese in 1921, but the ratio among the Indians had increased to 5.03 to 1. But these ratios were still very high at the end of this period when one considers that these figures in-clude the children born in Malaya, among whom the ratio of males to females would be approximately one to one.

The quadrupling of Singapore's population in the first fifty years after 1871 will have been more than duplicated during the second span of fifty years, but perhaps the most striking fact about the trend during this later period is that the relative size of the major racial elements has remained fairly constant, despite the important political and social crises which have occurred in the mean-time. The further increase in the proportion of Chinese since 1921 has been slight as compared with what happened in the previous hundred years. The

16

major effect of the data in Table 1, however, is to further confirm the evidence of Singapore's character as the meeting place of immigrants and the descendants of immigrants.

What has occurred most strikingly to Singapore's population during the period since 1921 has been the conversion of an essentially immigrant people into settled Singaporeans. At the beginning of the period Singapore consisted overwhelmingly (69.0 percent) of persons who had been born outside of Malaya. This situation had not changed greatly even by 1931 when 61.0 percent of the people on the island were still immigrants in the sense of having been born outside of any part of Malaya, including Singapore. As a consequence of the worldwide depression in the early 1930s, further immigration of men to Malaya was for the first time severely restricted in 1932, and this had the effect of causing the residents of Singapore to hesitate about returning to their native communities, lest there be difficulties in securing entrance to the colony a second time. There were no restrictions on the immigration of women until 1938, and shiploads of female passengers continued to arrive, thus reducing the sex disproportions among the immigrants and encouraging the establishment of families and permanent homes among them in the new environment. By

17

Table 1
Racial Composition of Singapore, 1871–1966

Race	1871	1901	1921	1931	1947	1957	1966
Malaysian	26,148 (26.9)	36,080 (15.8)	53,595 (12.8)	65,014 (11.6)	113,803 (12.1)	197,059 (13.6)	233,997 (12.1)
Chinese	54,572 (56.2)	164,041 (71.8)	315,151 (75.3)	418,640 (75.1)	729,473 (77.8)	1,090,596 (75.4)	1,519,225 (78.7)
Indian and Pakistani	10,754 (11.1)	17,823 (7.8)	32,314 (7.7)	50,811 (9.1)	68,967 (7.3)	124,084 (8.6)	128,250* (6.6)*
European	1,946 (2.0)	3,824 (1.7)	6,206 (1.4)	8,125 (1.5)	9,279 (1.0)	10,826 (.7)	48,261# (2.5)#
Eurasian	2,164 (2.0)	4,120 (1.8)	5,436 (1.3)	6,903 (1.2)	9,110 (1.0)	11,382 (.8)	
Others	1,527 (1.6)	2,667 (1.2)	6,656 (1.5)	8,252 (1.5)	7,512 (.8)	11,982 (.8)	
Total	97,111 (100.0)	228,555 (100.0)	418,358 (100.0)	557,745 (100.0)	938,144 (100.0)	1,445,929 (100.0)	1,929,733 (100.0)

Note: Numerals in parentheses indicate percentages.
* Includes Ceylonese, who previously had been included under "Others."
# The 1966 population survey combined Europeans and Eurasians under "Others."

1947 well over half of Singapore's residents (56.1 percent) were natives of the island and by 1966 nearly three-quarters (73.7 percent) of its total population had been born there.

The disposition of the immigrants to take root in Singapore has varied considerably from one racial group to another, depending upon factors too numerous and involved to analyze here. As one would expect, the Malaysian residents of Singapore have always had the highest proportion of their number who were born in Malaya, reaching 94.0 percent in 1966, but by 1957, the Chinese were already natives of Singapore to a higher degree (67.8 percent) than any of the other racial groups enumerated in that census, except the Eurasians. The proportion of native born, that is, born in Singapore, ranged as follows among the non-Chinese: Eurasian, 76.0 percent; Malaysian, 63.2 percent; Others (Arab, Nepalese, Jews, Filipinos, etc.), 61.7 percent; Ceylonese, 45.5 percent; Indians and Pakistani, 38.4 percent; and Europeans, 17.1 percent. According to the 1966 enumeration, the proportion of the population born in Singapore had reached 77.6 percent among the Chinese, 73.6 percent among the Malaysians, 58.7 percent among the Indians and Pakistani, and 31.7 percent among all other races. Presumably there has been a further increase of these ratios among all the major racial groups in the period since 1966.

There are, of course, many different factors which affect the ability and disposition of immigrant groups to sink permanent roots in the lands to which they have first been drawn simply to gain a livelihood. Of the tremendous flood of overseas migrants to Singapore since 1819,[13] only a fraction settled permanently on the island. Unquestionably the great majority of those coming as immigrants from the crowded peasant villages of Asia looked upon Singapore as only a temporary haven from which they might be able to gain at least the means of survival for a while and hopefully also to accumulate a surplus to make possible a permanent return to their homeland. Thousands of the immigrants to Singapore, who were subsequently distributed among the plantations and mines of Malaya, died there because of the unhealthy living conditions which prevailed during the early stages of their development; and there is no means of knowing how many of those who survived were able to realize their hopes of returning permanently to their ancestral villages.

Occupational Adjustment

Probably the two most critical factors which affected the number and selection of those who re-

20

mained and settled permanently were the market

demands for various skills on the immigrant fron-

tier and the ability and disposition of the immi-

grants to meet these demands. The first and fore-

most of these demands was for simple, untrained

animal strength and doggedness which these peasants

could provide, and it was, of course, in exchange

for this service as laborers in the mines and

plantations of the Malay Peninsula or on the ships,

wharves, godowns, or streets of Singapore that most

of the immigrants were able to survive during the

early period of their sojourn. Whether or not the

newcomers continued to remain in Singapore depended

to a considerable degree upon their willingness to

remain as scantily rewarded toilers in an alien

environment and upon their ability and disposition

to perform any of the wider range of skills for

which there are demands in such a trading center.

The one type of occupational adjustment, among

immigrants generally, which has been most widely

noted and commented about, especially with reference

to the Chinese, is the use of trade as an avenue

of escape from the monotony and drudgery of un-

skilled labor in the overseas communities to which

they have migrated. Trade, by its basic nature as

an impersonal exchange relationship, is peculiarly

suited to the circumstances of the outsiders and

strangers in any community, and despite an ignorance of the language or the customs of those
with whom he deals, it is possible for the newcomer
to secure an acceptable and profitable source of
livelihood in the marketplace, if he has any experience or inclination in that direction. Certain
Chinese, particularly from the coastal communities
of South China, had acquired over the centuries
considerable facility in trade in overseas areas
throughout Southeast Asia, and merchants from
Malacca were, along with the laborers, among the
first Chinese immigrants to Singapore in 1819.

European commentators on the social life in
Singapore, with few exceptions from Raffles down to
the present day, have felt impelled to write about
the manner and extent to which the immigrants--
notably the Chinese--have either come as traders
or have progressed from coolie laborer to itinerant
peddler and perhaps to merchant prince within a few
years of their arrival. Raffles himself was disposed to show special favoritism to the Chinese
merchants in Singapore in 1822 by granting them preferred areas of settlement in the new community,
stating that "the object of the Government being to
afford the utmost accommodation to every description of traders, but more particularly to the
respectable classes."[14] Both Western and Oriental

22

historians record that the merchant class was most encouraged by the British administration and was most successful in the eyes of the immigrant community. Song Ong Siang's notable history of the first one hundred years of the Singapore Chinese is heavily weighted with the biographical accounts of persons who had become merchants and whose influence had then extended into many other related areas, such as health, charities, education, and religion.

The frequent reference to the overseas Chinese as "the Jews of the Orient" is as inaccurate and misleading as most racial stereotypes, but like many such sweeping generalizations it does call attention to a significant trend in public thinking, of which some account must be taken. The fact is that, without a knowledge of the accepted ways of the country to which he has migrated or relatives or friends to assist him, the immigrant frequently has no available means of gaining a livelihood except trade, unless he is willing to remain as an unskilled laborer. Moreover, as an adventurer, daring enough to break the bonds to his family and home community, the immigrant is better prepared by temperament to take the risks inherent in trade than are the natives of the region.

Thus, as in other commercial centers of the world, in Singapore it has been the migrants from

23

the greater distances and facing a heavier personal
hazard--the Chinese and the Indians rather than the
Malaysians--who have most frequently entered into
the trading occupations. As the earlier arrivals,
the Chinese have invaded this field to a greater
degree than the Indians, but both groups have been
somewhat disproportionately employed in commercial
and financial occupations both at a lowly level
as "vendors, peddlers and hawkers" and as "proprietors and managers" of more remunerative establishments. Data derived from official census reports
amply confirm this widely held impression, but they
also indicate just as clearly that the vast majority
of the immigrants and their children derive their
livelihood from noncommercial occupations.

For purposes of illustration, the returns from
the 1947 census lend themselves more effectively
than those from earlier or later reports, but the
same general trends are apparent throughout the
present century. Thus, although the Chinese constituted 70.7 percent of the total male, employed
population of Singapore in that year, their proportion of those engaged in "commercial and financial occupations" made up 83.2 percent of the total,
or roughly 18 percent more than would have been
expected on the basis of equal representation among
all the racial groups. On the other hand, these
24

data certainly do not support the notion that the Chinese have monopolized the commercial and financial occupations. Within the lowest bracket of commercial occupations--as hawkers or vendors--the Chinese were overrepresented by a quarter, having 88.2 percent of all persons engaged in this field. At a higher level, as proprietors and managers of commercial establishments, the Chinese were again overrepresented, but only by one-eighth, or 12.9 percent. At this level, it was the Europeans who were most disproportionately so engaged, with more than two and a half times the expected number of proprietors and managers, whereas there were none engaged as vendors or hawkers.

The small group of "Others" noted in the census, consisting chiefly of Ceylonese, Arabian, and Nepalese immigrants and a few Jews, had roughly a fifth more than their proportionate number of males engaged in commercial and financial occupations, and as proprietors and managers their overrepresentation was considerably higher than among the Chinese, amounting to 80 percent. The Indians, on the other hand, who made up the second largest group of economically active males in 1947, were still overly confined to unskilled labor. Consequently they were short by slightly more than a tenth of their expected number in the large category of commercial and financial occupations, although almost exactly the number of Indians had become proprietors or managers of commercial establishments, which the size of their group might suggest.

The situation among the Malay and Other Malaysian males was, of course, quite different from that of the immigrant groups and reflected a very marked underrepresentation in the commercial occupations. Among the Malays proper, that is, those born in Malaya, there were less than one-eighth of the number in commercial pursuits that would have been expected on the basis of the total number of the economically active males, whereas among the Other Malaysians, those coming from outside Malaya, the proportion so engaged was somewhat higher, but still only about a quarter of the number that a group of that size might normally be expected to provide.

Data derived from the census nearly twenty years later (1966), despite unfortunate alterations of the categories utilized, reveal essentially the same relative status of the major racial groups with reference to this occupational field. By this time the Indians and Pakistani had improved their overall occupational status so as to have slightly more (1.2 percent) than an equal representation in the rather large category of what was then known as

26

"sales workers," but they were also overrepresented by a tenth as "working proprietors." The Chinese, to a lesser degree than the Indians, had also improved their position as sales workers and as working proprietors during this interval, resulting in an overrepresentation of approximately one-fifth in both categories. It is perhaps equally significant that the Chinese also continued to have a disproportionately high ratio in the less lucrative or preferred level of sales workers, as street and news vendors and canvassers. The Malay group, which also included in 1966 those classified as Other Malaysians in 1947, had a somewhat higher ratio of males engaged as sales workers or as proprietors of trading establishments than earlier, but it was still only about a third of what might have been expected if they were proportionally represented with the other racial groups. These sharp differences in occupational status between the Chinese, as the major immigrant group, and the Malays, who tend to think of themselves and are in many respects more fully indigenous to the region, constitute an inevitable source of racial friction which an equalitarian governmental policy and a generally favorable social atmosphere cannot completely disguise.

Trade and commerce have provided, of course,

only one of many channels by which the newcomers to Singapore have become established occupationally and economically, although it is also clear that the wealth created through trade has enabled the children and other relatives of these newcomers to obtain the necessary education and training for the many other preferred occupational careers. Quite understandably the histories of the Chinese in Singapore are chiefly preoccupied, during the greater part of the nineteenth century, with the accounts of immigrants who had been successful as merchants and among whom a primary concern had been to educate their children, particularly their sons, to continue and, if possible, to enhance the prestige and power of the family enterprise. This implied, of course, the enjoyment of the benefits resulting from the possession of wealth, such as the honors associated with the donations to charities, public monuments, hospitals, and educational institutions, as well as indulging in lavish entertainment, horse racing, and other forms of prestigious recreation.

Toward the end of the last century there were beginning to be numerous references to immigrants who were themselves utilizing the leisure, made possible by their accumulation of wealth in commerce, for the cultivation of intellectual and artistic skills of various sorts, and who also en-

couraged their children and grandchildren to obtain the Western education requisite for careers
as doctors, lawyers, dentists, scientists, and other
professions. There were already by the end of the
century a number of Western-trained Chinese lawyers
and doctors practicing in Singapore, and by the time
of the census in 1947, nearly half of the enumerated physicians and surgeons were Chinese and
another fifth were either Indians or of other immigrant communities. The proportion of the immigrants from Asia or their descendants engaged in
this prestigious occupation was still very much
lower than their ratio of all the "economically
active" persons in the entire population, but considering the humble origins from which many of
them--either they or their kinsmen--had emerged,
the advancement along this occupational channel
had been very considerable. By contrast, the
Malays and Other Malaysians were scarcely represented at all.

In the legal professions--as judges, magis-
trates, and lawyers--the ascent of the immigrants
has been considerably slower. This is a consequence in part of the dominant role occupied by
the Europeans and Eurasians, who, perhaps in conformity with the colonial policy of the day, together made up 54 percent of those in the profession

although they constituted only 2 percent of the economically active population in 1947. The Chinese had only a little more than a third (36.5 percent) of the number which could have been expected on the basis of the size of the group, while the Indians had nearly three-fourths (72.7 percent) of their expected number. Again, however, the Malays and Other Malaysians were grossly underrepresented, with less than one-sixth of the number which might have been assumed.

By 1957 the two major immigrant groups had further improved their positions in the professional fields, although neither of them to the point where they closely approximated their expected number in all areas. The Chinese had already surpassed their assumed ratio as physicians, surgeons, dentists, and medical specialists, as teachers (except at the university level), and as actors and other skilled entertainers. The Indians and Pakistanis were still below par in all these areas, but had exceeded their expected number as draftsmen, cartographers, and other science and engineering technicians. The Malaysians were still markedly underrepresented in almost all professional fields but contributed con-siderably more than their expected proportion of musicians and actors and other skilled entertainers, while the category of Other Races, consisting

30

chiefly of Europeans and Eurasians, had two or more times the expected number in all major professional fields, except that of actors and skilled entertainers.

Much the same trends as those already noted continued well into the 1960s, with many, although certainly not all, in the immigrant groups moving further into the more lucrative and preferred occupations, but with the Malays tending to lag markedly behind in this process. A rough indication is provided of the extent to which the major racial groups had been able or disposed to establish themselves in a fairly broad range of occupations in Singapore. These data are obtained from the findings from the Singapore Sample Household Survey of 1966 and are best suited for presentation in four broad classes of occupation on the basis of whether the specific racial group had:

0. no male representation,

1. less than half of the number of male participants that could be expected on the basis of the group's total economically active male population,

2. more than half but not its entire number of expected male participants, or,

3. more than its expected number of male participants.[15]

	Chinese	Malay	Indian or Pakistani	Other Races (European, Eurasian, etc.)
Professional, technical				
a. Engineers	2	0	2	3
b. Drafts-men	3	0	1	3
c. Physicians, surgeons, and medical specialists	3	0	1	0
d. Teachers (primary and secondary)	3	2	3	3
e. Actors, musicians, dancers, etc.	2	3	0	1
Administrators, executives, and managers				
f. government administrators	2	2	3	3
g. Directors, managers, proprietors (except in trade)	3	1	2	3

	Chinese	Malay	Indian or Pakistani	Other Races (European, Eurasian, etc.)
Clerical and related workers				
h. Book-keepers and cashiers	3	1	2	3
i. Clerical workers	3	2	2	3
Sales workers				
j. Working proprie-tors in trade	3	1	3	1
k. Street vendors	3	1	2	1
Craftsmen				
l. Tailors	3	1	2	0
m. Jewelers	3	0	2	2
n. Machin-ists and tool-makers	3	2	1	3
o. Plumbers, welders, platers	3	2	3	1
p. Carpen-ters, joiners, cabinet-makers	3	1	1	1
q. Painters and pa-perhang-ers	3	1	2	0

33

	Chinese	Malay	Indian or Pakistani	Other Races (European, Eurasian, etc.)
Service workers				
r. Police	2	3	3	2
s. Armed forces	1	3	3	3
t. Watchmen	1	3	3	1
u. Street cleaners and gar-bage men	2	3	3	1
v. Barbers, hair-dressers, etc.	2	1	3	1
Agriculture and fishery workers				
w. Agricul-ture work-ers	3	1	1	0
x. Fishermen	3	3	0	0
Laborers				
y. Miscel-laneous	3	3	2	1
z. Sailors, barge crews, and boatmen	2	3	1	0

The foregoing data, representing half of the economically active male population of Singapore in 1966, give further support to the proposition that the initiative which led peasants of China, India,

34

and Ceylon to tear loose from their native soil in search of a better livelihood overseas may also enable them to climb higher on the economic scale in their adopted land. Such upward mobility of an extensive nature and especially in its more dramatic forms—from farm laborer to government administrator, or from street vendor to surgeon—was neither possible nor universally sought by the immigrants or their children. More than a generation after the closing of further immigration, the lowlier occupations in terms of remuneration and prestige were still chiefly supplied by the immigrants or their descendants.

The failure of the Malays to penetrate the more skilled and supposedly preferred occupations to anything like the same degree as the Chinese, Indians, or Europeans need not be attributed to a lack of ability on the part of the Malays, but it would seem rather to be a consequence of an absence of motivation in the direction of monetary achievements. For the great majority of the Malays the simple scale of living in association with kinfolk in the kampong[16] brought greater happiness and serenity of mind and spirit and was preferred to any material advantages, which participation in the endless striving of a competitive economy might possibly provide them. Even the Malays who had mi-

35

grated from Indonesia could find in Singapore a congenial atmosphere in which the customs and community relationships of their native village could be largely reestablished.

It is reasonable to assume, on the other hand, that the heavy representation of the "Other Races," consisting chiefly of Europeans and Eurasians, in the so-called preferred occupations, such as professional, administrative, and proprietary, is in part a carry-over into the 1960s of racial patronage and privilege, dating from colonial days.

Notes

1. Harry Miller, The Story of Malaysia (London, 1965), pp. 72, 74-75.

2. Singapore Year Book 1967 (Singapore, 1968), p. 37.

3. Ibid.

4. Ibid.

5. Guy Hunter, Southeast Asia: Race, Culture, and Nation (London, 1966), p. 14.

6. United Nations Yearbook of National Accounts Statistics (New York, 1968).

7. Ooi Jin-Bee, "Singapore: The Balance-Sheet," in Ooi Jin-Bee and Chiang Hai Ding (editors), Modern Singapore (Singapore, 1969), pp. 1-13.

8. Victor Purcell, The Chinese in Malaya (Longon, 1967), p. 8

9. Quoted in Victor Purcell, The Chinese in Malaya (London, 1967), pp. 70-71.

10. *Ibid.*, p. 88.

11. *Singapore Year Book 1967* (Singapore, 1968), p. 39.

12. *Ibid.*

13. From China alone, it is estimated that no less than six million immigrants arrived in Singapore between 1895 and 1927, reaching an all time record of 360,000 in a single year. Donald and Joanna Moore, *The First 150 Years of Singapore* (Singapore, 1969), p. 491.

14. Song Ong Siang, *One Hundred Years' History of the Chinese in Singapore* (Singapore, 1967), p. 10.

15. A brief explanation of the method by which these data were obtained is provided in Appendix A.

16. The Malay term for village or small settlement, which has been widely adopted by other immigrant groups throughout Malaysia.

ETHNIC, RACIAL, AND POLITICAL FACTORS
IN SINGAPORE'S DEVELOPMENT

The immigrant groups in Singapore have been discussed, up to this point, as if they constituted
homogeneous ethnic units. The overwhelming majority
of the people--close to 80 percent--are recorded in
the census and in most of the official statistics
under a single racial category, Chinese. So also
another eighth of the population are officially
categorized as Malaysians in contrast to still
another sixteenth who are listed as Indians and
Pakistanis. A residual collection of Europeans,
Eurasians, Ceylonese, Nepalese, Thai, Filipinos,
Japanese, and a score of other ethnic representatives, making up about 2.5 percent of the population, are banded together under a blanket term of
Other Races, indicating the heterogeneous nature
of this one term.

Ethnic Groups within the Races

The very term race,[1] as applied to the immigrant
groups in Singapore, is a creation by the residents
of the island, specifically by the British colonial
authorities, with reference to the newcomers, and
it reflects therefore the British designations and

classifications of the immigrants rather than the
ones used by the immigrants themselves. Since
racial labels are always devices for indicating and
preserving social distances among identifiable
groups, they tend to follow social usage and custom
in the dominating power structure, and, hence, the
ethnic realities within the subordinate immigrant
groups are commonly unknown or overlooked by those
in power.

Chinese. The British authorities in Singapore, from
Raffles, Farquhar, and Crawford down to William
Goode, could not fail to recognize marked differences in physical appearance, language, custom, and
occupational capabilities between Indians, for
example, and the Chinese, but there were no apparent
reasons for taking account of the distinctions of
this type which either the Indians or the Chinese
made among themselves, however important these
might be to them. Raffles, however, as early as
1822 in establishing a plan for the orderly development of the community, felt compelled in the case
of the Chinese "to advert to the provincial and
other distinctions among this peculiar people." It
had already been called to his attention that there
were significant differences in temperament among
them such that "continued disputes and disturbances
take place between people of different provinces."[2]

With his concern primarily upon the economic capabilities of the immigrants, Raffles was disposed
in assigning areas of residence in the community to
give special consideration "to every description of
traders, but more particularly to the respectable
classes," which he evidently assumed were drawn
preponderantly from among the Chinese from Amoy
Hokkiens. The "lower classes of Chinese . . . those
gaining their livelihood by handicrafts and personal
labour," and the cultivators presumably deserved
less attention in the allotment of land and might
justifiably be removed from areas they had already
occupied so as to provide those "engaged in mercantile speculation" with preferred locations.[3]

This form of residential segregation, institu-
ted by the colonial authorities almost at the outset of the Singapore settlement, tended to re-
enforce the language and other cultural barriers
which inevitably isolate the various immigrant
groups from one another and from the classes in
authority. Hence it was natural that only the
merchant class, whose livelihood depends upon contact and communication with the outside community,
should have become known to the authorities as a
distinct ethnic subgroup within the "Chinese race."[4]
The outbreak of riots among the Chinese toward the
end of 1824, in which "several persons were killed

40

and wounded,"[5] gave further intimation of the existence of distinct and conflicting groups within this immigrant community. Even the official historian of the first century of the Chinese in Singapore, however, did not regard such an event as sufficiently significant to record what the opposing groups or the issues involved were. It was not until a good many years later that there was any official, much the less any widespread public, recognition of any need to penetrate beyond the barriers to human understanding and association which are involved in such broad and impersonal classifications as Chinese, Malay, Indian, or Arab. Outsiders, such as missionaries, government administrators, and traders working directly with the immigrants soon became aware of important group distinctions within these large categories and learned to adjust their conduct accordingly. However, some major explosion of conflict across ethnic lines within a so-called racial group, such as the disastrous riot of 1854 in which Teochews were pitted against Hokkienese and at least four hundred persons were killed,[6] seemed to be required to bring about any widespread public awareness that the people within the immigrant groups were not all alike and that many distinct and possibly conflicting subgroups might also exist. Obviously, however, such destructive expressions would hardly have led to increased appreciation or understanding among ethnic or racial groups. So also the discovery that mutual-aid and secret political societies existed within the immigrant groups and were taking justice into their own hands, using violent methods in the enforcement of their rules, served to further intensify, rather than to diminish, the barriers of race.

During the second half of the nineteenth century some of the major group distinctions within the so-called racial groups had become sufficiently apparent in the wider community as to encourage some of the official agencies to break away from the blanket terms previously used and to take some account of the ethnic or dialectal groupings within such categories as Chinese and Indian. The data in Table 2 reflect the earlier and cumulatively greater influx of the three major "tribal" groups among the Chinese, of which the Hokkiens, originally from the vicinity of Amoy, were the first to migrate extensively to Malaysia and to become most firmly established as residents (Babas) and in the more lucrative occupations.[7] It is quite possible that their early reputation for being "quarrelsome" resulted in part from the resistance they demonstrated toward the invasion of their established positions

42

in shopkeeping and mercantile occupations by the later-arriving Teochews from around Swatow and by the Cantonese, many of whom had prior experience as tradesmen.

Although the tabular data provide no substantiating support, the 1931 Census reported that "the Cantonese appear to be more versatile, or catholic in their taste in the way of occupation and mode of life, than the Hokkiens," and the 1947 Census gave much the same impression. The statistical data from the census, however, which most strikingly distinguished the Cantonese from all other ethnic groups among the Chinese, revealed a relatively high proportion of females as compared to males, reaching 841 per thousand males by 1931 and climbing to 1,230 per thousand males in 1957. The Cantonese are the only subgroup among the Chinese in which there has ever been an excess of females, and to whom the other groups have turned for wives. The Hainanese, fourth largest of the Chinese ethnic groups in Singapore, on the other hand, have been least adequately supplied with women, owing to governmental restrictions upon their emigration from Hainan. Toward the beginning of the period for which census data for the separate Chinese ethnic groups were available (1881), there were only 6.4 Hainanese females per thousand males and

Table 2

The Chinese Population of Singapore by Ethnic Groups

Ethnic Group	1891	1901	1931	1947	1957
Hokkien	45,856 (37.6)	59,117 (36.0)	180,108 (42.9)	289,109 (39.6)	442,707 (40.6)
Teochew	23,737 (19.5)	27,564 (16.8)	82,405 (19.6)	157,186 (21.6)	245,190 (22.5)
Cantonese	23,397 (19.2)	30,729 (18.7)	94,742 (22.6)	157,598 (21.6)	205,773 (18.9)
Hainanese	8,711 (7.1)	9,451 (5.8)	19,896 (4.7)	52,117 (7.1)	78,081 (7.2)
Hakka (Kheh)	7,402 (6.1)	8,514 (5.2)	19,317 (4.6)	39,988 (5.5)	73,072 (6.7)
Foochow (Hokchiu)	-- (--)	12,888* (7.9)*	6,539 (1.6)	9,461 (1.3)	16,828 (1.5)
Henghua	-- (--)	-- (--)	n.a. (n.a.)	7,445 (1.0)	8,757 (0.8)
Hokchia	-- (--)	-- (--)	8,840 (2.1)	6,323 (0.9)	7,614 (0.7)

Table 2 (continued)

Ethnic Group	1891	1901	1931	1947	1957
Kwongsai	-- (--)	-- (--)	945 (0.2)	681 (0.1)	292 (--)
Shanghainese	-- (--)	-- (--)	n.a. (n.a.)	n.a. (n.a.)	11,034 (1.0)
Straits born	12,805 (10.5)	15,498 (9.5)	n.a. (n.a.)	n.a. (n.a.)	n.a. (n.a.)
Other and Indeterminate	-- (--)	280 (0.2)	6,772 (1.6)	9,565 (1.3)	1,248 (0.1)
Total	121,908 (100.0)	164,041 (100.0)	419,564 (100.0)	729,473 (100.0)	1,090,596 (100.0)

Sources: Data for 1891 and 1901 from Hayes Marriott, "The Peoples of Singapore," in Walter Makepeace, ed., One Hundred Years of Singapore (Longon, 1921), p. 362. Data for 1931 from C. A. Vlieland, A Report on the 1931 Census, British Malaya (London, 1932), p. 181. Data for 1947 and 1957 from S. C. Chua, Report on the Census of Population, 1957, State of Singapore (Singapore, 1964), p. 68.

Note: Numerals in parentheses indicate percentages.

* This figure undoubtedly includes a considerable number of Hokkien and probably some Henghua and Hokchia.

even as late as 1957 there were still only 777 per thousand males, as compared with 963 for the entire Chinese population of Singapore. The Hainanese have been credited by the earlier census reports (1931 and 1947) with a preference for and being mainly engaged in domestic service, and later accounts indicate a similar specialization as domestic servants and as sailors but also some tendency to push into more remunerative trades and skilled occupations.

The fifth largest of the major Chinese ethnic groups, the Hakkas or Khehs, differed from the others in not being identified with any one specific geographic area of South China. This was a consequence of their having been the victims of a long series of forced migrations beginning as early as the third century B.C., and fierce struggles occurred for a place to live among the residents of the areas of South China into which they have been compelled to move. There has obviously been a certain carry-over of these tensions to the overseas areas, which has particularly affected the role which the Hakkas have been able to play in Singapore. According to the earlier census reports, the Hakkas were "probably the most rurally inclined of all the tribes and . . . are also widely engaged in agricultural pursuits,"[8] but in the colony of Singa-

46

pore, the Hakkas were already more highly concentrated in the municipality or the urbanized areas than was true of the Chinese population as a whole. Although the Hakkas, like the Hainanese, were especially known to have arrived in Singapore at the penniless or "Sinkhek" level and made their initial occupational adjustment at unskilled or semiskilled occupations, a significant proportion have since come to be preponderantly identified with more profitable occupations. Among the latter are the operation of such establishments as pawnshops, iron foundries, shirtmaking, shoe and tailoring shops, tin and zinc manufacture, textile and cloth merchandising.

The other ethnic subgroups among the Chinese are much fewer in numbers, and in comparison with the large mass among the five groups mentioned, they tend much less frequently to stand out or to be recognized as distinct social entities.

Indians. The disposition to take account of ethnic distinctions among the Indians also dates back to the latter part of the nineteenth century, but because the numbers involved are much smaller than among the Chinese and the large influx of Indians has occurred more recently, the differences have frequently emerged less sharply in public consciousness. There had obviously been some Indian traders in Singapore almost from its founding, since 753 were listed in an enumeration in 1823, but the total number of Indians in the population continued to be less than 10,000 until the second half of the century, and it was not until after 1880 that any large number of Indians pushed on into Singapore after completing their labor contracts on the rubber estates in Malaya. The massive increase in the Indian population of Singapore occurred after the beginning of the twentieth century, mounting from 17,000 or 7.8 percent of the total in 1901 to nearly twice that figure (32,342) in 1921, and continuing rapidly upward to 128,250 in 1966.

The initial and largest number among the ethnic subgroups to become clearly distinguishable within the Indian community in Singapore, as elsewhere in Malaya, were the Tamils from South India and Ceylon, most of whom had been recruited originally for labor on the plantations and estates of the region and later moved into the city. By 1921, the Tamils constituted nearly four-fifths of all Indians in Singapore, and although their proportion declined somewhat in later years they were still in 1957 much the largest of the Indian subgroups on the island (see Table 3). In fact, the Tamils had come to occupy so prominent a place in the Indian community, not only in Singapore but throughout Malaya,

48

Table 3
Indian and Pakistani Population by Ethnic Groups

Ethnic Group	1931	1947	1957
Tamil	37,231 (73.2)	42,240 (61.2)	78,228 (63.0)
Malayali	4,378 (8.6)	9,712 (14.1)	21,783 (17.6)
Punjabi	5,236 (10.3)	3,551 (5.2)	7,757 (6.3)
Sikh	n.a. (n.a.)	2,196 (3.2)	3,405 (2.7)
Bengali	1,166 (2.3)	1,253 (1.8)	2,405 (1.9)
Other and Indeterminate	2,873 (5.6)	10,015 (14.5)	10,506 (8.5)
Total	50,884 (100.0)	68,967 (100.0)	124,084 (100.0)

Sources: C. A. Vlieland, A Report on the 1931 Census, British Malaya (London, 1932), p. 193; and S. C. Chua, Report on the Census of Population, 1957, State of Singapore (Singapore, 1964), p. 70.

Note: Numerals in parentheses indicate percentages.

that it was said in the 1931 report of the Census in British Malaya:

> As to race, most Asiatics in Malaya, and certainly the vast majority of those available as enumerators, only recognize two classes of Indians--i.e. "Klings" or southern Indians of whom the Tamil is taken as a type, and "Bengalis" including all others.[9]

This tendency in the wider community to differentiate only between the South Indian "Klings," com-

49

monly identified as Tamils, and North Indians has
been attributed to indifference toward the Indian
minority, and the term "Kling" has become offensive
as reflecting contempt. Actually the Malayalis,
who now make up nearly a fifth of the total Indian
community, are also from South India (the Malabar
Coast) and they differ significantly from the
Tamils in possessing larger physiques and they were
consequently employed more extensively in dock and
heavy industrial labor.

Although the majority of the South Indian
immigrants to Singapore came as laborers, many of
the later arrivals were educationally qualified to
take positions at middle-class and professional
levels, but as outsiders or recent arrivals it was
not uncommon for them to accept work in clerical and
other pursuits with considerably less recognition
and compensation than their capabilities might justify. South Indian Muslim traders and Tamil Chet-
tyars, as moneylenders, financiers, and business
promoters, also served to modify somewhat the
earlier stereotype of Tamils and Malayalis as unskilled laborers.

The North Indian immigrants and their Singa-
pore-born children were readily distinguished from
those originating in South India on the basis of
their lighter complexion, distinctive dress, es-

pecially among the men, and their occupations. Punjabis, Sikhs, and Bengalese were recruited by the government and private business for police, defense, and general security purposes and as "technical personnel on the railways,"[10] and others came on their own initiative to find openings in skilled labor, mercantile, and professional occupations. Except for the relatively small Bengali community, most of the North Indians in Singapore appear to have become more firmly established in the Singapore community than those from South India. The abnormalities of a shifting, unsettled society--a great excess of adult men over women, running as high as ten to one in some age classes, and bearing its inevitable consequences in an absence of family life--were strikingly apparent among both Tamils and Malayalis as recently as 1957.

In contrast to the Chinese, the ethnic groups among the Indians have given little evidence of the deep-seated tensions, for example, such as those which once existed between Hokkiens and Teochews. Probably the nearest approximation was the strain between Muslims and Hindus, but with over 80 percent of Singapore's Indians being Hindus, there has been little disposition to make an issue of religious differences.

Malaysians. The major group distinctions among

the Malaysian immigrants, in contrast with those
among the Chinese and Indian immigrants, seem to have
been readily recognized, at least by Westerners, at
the very outset of extensive contacts after 1819,
whereas they have gradually faded in public consciousness with the passage of time. Even the earliest accounts by Westerners mention the Bugis
traders from the Celebes as distinct from the indigenous Malays,[11] and references were soon made to
settled agricultural communities of Javanese and
Bugis, but situated some distance from "a large
village occupied exclusively by Malays, few of whom
apparently follow any occupation, though some guess
may be made respecting their mode of procuring
substance."[12] The Javanese and Bugis settlers along
the coast and on the small "islets off the harbor"
were supposedly known for their bravery in resisting
pirate attacks from still other Malays, possibly
from Sumatra.

Reference continued to be made to the flow of
groups of immigrants to Singapore from various parts
of the Malaysian archipelago and the Malay penin-
sula--people who were distinguishable on the basis
of language and custom, although most of them shared
a common Muslim religion. Beginning as early as
1825 the census reports distinguished between Bugis,
Malays, and Javanese, and by 1849 the Boyanese from
52

the vicinity of Madura were added to the list of
Other Malaysians.[13] At the time of the 1881 census,
a small number of Dyaks, Jawi Pekans, and a few
Filipinos, presumably from Mindanao, were also
separately listed as Malay races. Still others, including Achinese, Bataks, Menangkabaus, Korinichis,
Jambis, and Banjarese were added in later censuses,
with the larger groups continuing to be separately
listed in summary tables as late as 1957.

The observations on the Malaysians in the census of 1947, however, would suggest that these distinctions had already ceased to be of much more than
academic interest, not only in Singapore but
throughout the whole of Malaya.

> The distinction between the Malays and the
> Other Malaysians is not very great and is,
> indeed, ignored in the compilation of
> Malaya vital statistics; for the Malays
> themselves are, to a large extent, de-
> scended from the Malays of the East Coast
> of Sumatra from whom . . . they are ethno-
> graphically indistinguishable. . . . As
> for the Other Malaysian, all but a hand-
> ful of them are of the Muslim faith and
> speak the Malay language and are, though
> to varying degrees, readily assimilable
> with the Malays of the peninsula with
> whom, in fact, they tend to form a single
> community.[14]

One suspects that the earlier categories among the
Malays were retained in the later enumerations
(1947 and 1957), chiefly for the purposes of comparison. Even in 1931, the Superintendent of the
Census indicated that throughout British Malaya

Table 4

Malaysian Population of Singapore by Ethnic Groups

Ethnic Group	1849	1871	1901	1931	1947	1957
Malays	12,206 (72.3)	19,270 (73.7)	23,060 (63.9)	38,462 (58.1)	70,331 (61.8)	135,662 (68.8)
Javanese	1,649 (9.8)	3,240 (12.4)	8,519 (23.6)	15,958 (24.1)	24,679 (21.7)	36,009 (18.3)
Boyanese	763 (4.5)	1,634 (6.2)	2,712 (7.5)	9,407 (14.2)	15,394 (13.5)	22,167 (11.3)
Bugis	2,269 (13.4)	1,996 (7.6)	999 (2.8)	793 (1.2)	705 (0.6)	1,069 (0.5)
Dyaks	-- (--)	1 (--)	29 (0.1)	44 (0.1)	-- (--)	-- (--)
Jawi Pekans	-- (--)	-- (--)	665 (1.8)	-- (--)	-- (--)	-- (--)
Filipinos	-- (--)	7 (--)	94 (--)	-- (--)	-- (--)	-- (--)

Table 4 (continued)

Ethnic Group	1849	1871	1901	1931	1947	1957
Banjarese	-- (--)	-- (--)	-- (--)	416 (0.6)	-- (--)	-- (--)
Other	-- (--)	-- (--)	2 (--)	1,092 (1.7)	2,694 (2.4)	1,248 (1.1)
Total	16,887 (100.0)	26,148 (100.0)	36,080 (100.0)	66,172 (100.0)	113,803 (100.0)	197,059 (100.0)

Note: Numerals in parentheses indicate percentages.

the distinctions among the Malaysians had largely broken down--that although the children born in Malaya of Javanese, Boyanese, Banjarese, or Dyak immigrant parents would normally be classified in the "race" of their parents, "the children born in Malaya of Sumatran parents are normally returned as 'Malay.'"

> This procedure is designed to reflect the persistence of separate race consciousness, customs and language in the case of Javanese and other immigrant peoples from the south and west of the archipelago, as contrasted with the ready assimilation of the Sumatran Malay.[15]

He went on further to indicate that a somewhat detailed classification of the Malaysian immigrant groups was retained in the 1931 census in large part in response to political considerations between the Malayan and the Netherlands Indian governments.

An examination of the data in Table 4 reveals several other significant trends among the ethnic groups or "communities" within the so-called Malaysian race over a period of somewhat more than a century--from 1849 to 1957, for which census data are available. Of the four major groups, all except the Bugis have experienced a steady increase in numbers, with the two smaller immigrant groups-- the Javanese and the Boyanese--advancing proportionately much more rapidly than the Malays prior

56

to 1931 and much less so in the twenty-six years after. Throughout this initial 82-year period, the disproportion of males to females was always very much higher among the Javanese and the Boyanese than it was among either the Malays or the Bugis, and it is reasonable to assume that the single male immigrants sought wives from among the native Malays, with the result that their children were classified with their father's ethnic group, rather than with their mother's. In the period since 1931 there has been little further immigration, and the sex disproportions have largely disappeared, with the result that the ratio of Malays has increased and that of the non-Malays has declined. Thus, as a consequence of the integrating influence of a common Muslim religion and of common linguistic and customary patterns throughout the Malaysian archipelago, there has probably been less retention of separate ethnic consciousness within the Malaysian race than among either Indians or Chinese.

Europeans, Eurasians, and Others. The disposition on the part of some Western observers of the Singapore social scene to apply the term European as an all-embracing racial category to cover all those who either themselves or whose ancestors had migrated from any European country has resulted in oversights and inconsistencies no less glaring than the earlier tendency to regard as a single racial entity all those who had emigrated from China or from India. In the earliest census reports dating from 1821 to 1860, the single term European was used, followed usually but not always by separate categories for Indo-Britons or Eurasian, Native Christians, Armenians, and Jews. When these latter terms were not used, it is not always clear as to whether the persons previously so classified had left the island or were included in the term European. The number separately listed as Europeans reached its first high point of 141 out of a total population in the colony of just under 30,000 in 1836, and in 1849 there were 360 persons listed as Europeans out of a total population of 59,043. Beginning with the census of 1871, there was a general category for Europeans and Americans, divided functionally as to whether they were resident, floating, prisoners, or British military, but further differentiated among some 25 nationality or linguistic categories such as Americans, Bohemians, Danes, Hungarians, Rumanians, Turks, and West Indians. Eurasians were listed as a separate racial category, while Jews were included as a distinct grouping under Others, along with such groups as Africans, Japanese, Siamese, and Turks (Asiatic). This practice was followed more or less consistently

58

through the census report of 1947, when the caption, "Europeans and Other 'White' Communities" was utilized, emphasizing further the color distinction.

By 1957 the European population had been so greatly overshadowed in numbers by the other racial groups and the emphasis upon their significance during the colonial period had so far declined that it was no longer considered necessary to differentiate within this category, and by 1966 the Europeans were not separately listed at all, but simply included within the miscellaneous bracket of Other Races.

Neither the Europeans nor their mixed-blood offspring have ever figured very prominently numerically in the population of Singapore. Even in 1891, when they reached their highest proportion, together they made up only 4.8 percent of the total, and by 1957 this ratio had dropped to 1.5 percent. This, of course, is no indication whatever of their role in the economic and political life of the island in which the Europeans and most notably the British played an extremely prominent part until the time of the war in the Pacific—less prominently since then.

It would seem from the data in Table 5 that the British were most disposed among the Europeans to take advantage of the opportunities which Singapore offered as a developing commercial frontier—their

Table 5
The Population of Europeans, Eurasians,
and Other Races, 1849-1957

Races	1849	1871	1901	1931	1947	1957
Europeans	360	1,946	3,824	8,147	9,351	10,826
British		594	1,880	6,640	7,751	N.S.L.*
Eurasians	922	2,164	4,120	6,937	9,110	11,382
Arabs	194	466	919	1,939	2,588	3,471
Jews	22	57	462	777	877	729
Ceylonese		7	244	1,645	2,960	5,426
Japanese		1	766	3,215	45	194

*Not separately listed.

proportion of the European population there having

increased from 31.3 percent in 1871 to 83.0 percent

in 1947. It would also appear that the major

legacy of the Europeans to the future population

of Singapore, although still relatively small, is

likely to be their mixed-blood descendants, whose

number increased much more rapidly than among all

Europeans in the period from 1901 to 1957.

Certain "Other Races" or "Communities," as

they have been variously characterized in official

documents, were included in Table 5 because each,

despite its limited numbers, has performed a some-

what distinctive part in the life of the larger

Singapore community. For example, it was reported

in 1931 that of the small community of less than

two thousand Arabs in Singapore, in contrast with

the three thousand in the rest of British Malaya,
"the great majority . . . are of pure descent; some
of them are very wealthy, and they and the Jews
. . . are the largest owners of house property
/real estate/ in the town."[16] It is well known that
the Arabs have been conceived as something of an
aristocracy within the Muslim world and there has
been some disposition elsewhere in what was British
Malaya for Malays with "even a tincture of Arab
blood" to call themselves Arabs.

It is significant that the Jews have never been
listed in any of the census reports as Europeans,
and perhaps as a consequence of this isolation--at
least in part--it could also be said of them in
1947 that they were "a closely knit community, much
engaged in business, big and little."[17] Somewhat
more than nine-tenths (93.4 percent) of all the
Jews in British Malaya in 1931 were located in
Singapore.

The cultural and linguistic distinctions between the Sinhalese, who were engaged chiefly in
shopkeeping, and the Ceylon Tamils, occupied
earlier largely in clerical tasks, have not always
been fully recognized and have led to some incon-
sistency in census classification, with the latter
being included as Indians prior to 1931. The small
number of Japanese listed in the table, except in

1931, gives no adequate indication of their dominant role during the war years nor of their increasing significance in industry and commerce since 1957.

The Colonial Power Structure

Singapore had certainly figured prominently in the trading between distant parts of the Malaysian archipelago over centuries preceding the British occupation of the island as a strategic center for their expanding colonial empire, but it is the period since Raffles' daring venture in 1819 that the influences most relevant to the present and future situations have clearly emerged. The mention in Chinese trading accounts at the time of the Three Kingdoms (231 A.D.) of the "Pu-luo-chung" might very well refer to Singapore as "the island at the terminal end of a peninsula," but it has little bearing on the present-day scene, except as a possible matter of academic interest to Chinese scholars. Certainly there is little, except museum evidence, in today's world of the undoubted existence during the thirteenth and fourteenth centuries of successive Indian settlements, known as Temasek, since most of the island during the intervening five centuries was simply overrun by the jungle.

The island of Singapore is so closely associated by nature with the Malaysian peninsula that most

historians have found it impossible in dealing
with the economic and political development of the
region to discuss the experience of one without
also giving attention to the other, and a dominant
theme running through the historical accounts by
Europeans of both Singapore and Malaysia during the
period of colonial rule has been the civilizing and
materially elevating functions performed by the
British administrators and business promoters
under difficult circumstances. So, for example,
one of the more prolific and widely accepted of the
Western historians on the region simply combines
Malaysia and Singapore as the title of a summary
analysis of the political, social, and economic
background of the two states named.[18] From a preliminary depiction of a region, much of which remains as impenetrable a jungle in the twentieth
century A.D. as it was in the twentieth century
B.C., the account moves rapidly to the modernizing
influences brought to the region by the Portuguese,
and Dutch, in the seventeenth and eighteenth centuries, but reaching its climax under British rule
in the nineteenth and early twentieth centuries.

British control, first in the coastal trading
communities of Penang, Malacca, and Singapore, and
extending later throughout the interior of the
peninsula as well, was accepted, if not actually

welcomed by nearly all of the Malay community as the means of bringing order and stability to a region previously torn somewhat by racial tensions and political rivalries.

> The early British pioneers worked hard to establish law and order and to develop the state; in doing so, they secured the good-will and support of both Malay and Chinese . . . . they administered with a light, benevolent hand.[19]

The relatively mild forms of political restraint imposed by the British, conforming closely with their laissez faire policy in trade and of indirect rule in government, was apparently designed chiefly to prevent unnecessary violence and bloodshed and to facilitate the peaceful commercial activities for which the colony was primarily founded.

The positive contributions of British rule in Singapore, first under the British East India Company from 1819 to 1867 and following that as a Crown Colony until 1941, were expressed rather as the incidental by-products of trade promotion. The elimination of piracy on the land and sea approaches to Singapore, extending modern harbor facilities, an intricate system of roads and highways, and communication within the colony by telephone and with the outside world by wireless--these were pre-requisites for the advancing profits to the British promoters of the colony, but they also contributed

64

to the effective commercial relations and the material advancement of all who lived on the island, regardless of their nationality or racial origin. So also the historians contend that the introduction of Western technology and science for the production of agricultural crops and the extraction of minerals added substantially to the wealth, not only of the European entrepreneurs but of the native and immigrant laborers as well.

The establishment by the British of a uniform and clearly defined system of civil and criminal law, honestly and dispassionately enforced by the police and the courts, was a major contribution to the well-being of all Singapore's residents, which particularly impressed Western historians. British insistence on the abolition of a host of customary practices among both immigrants and natives but regarded by those in authority as barbaric or deleterious to human welfare, such as slavery, certain forms of gambling, the taking of private or communal vengeance, and the arbitrary exaction of taxes and duties by chiefs or headmen--such changes were simply taken for granted as self-evident gains.[20] The enforcement of basic rules governing public health and sanitation and the introduction of preventive and curative medicine, of course, have greatly reduced the incidence of the more serious diseases of the area and increased the longevity of the entire population, particularly during the present century.

It must be conceded, however, that governmental concern for the health of any but their British countrymen was relatively late in developing. The early hospitals established by the East India Company were designed for the troops brought to Singapore, although they also treated the European sick, but during the first half of the nineteenth century, the efforts of the government to deal with the health problems of the total population were chiefly confined to the meager facilities of a "poorhouse," for the benefit of "convict patients as well as town paupers and even European patients."[21] Actually the first hospital "for the diseased of all countries" was erected in 1844, not by the government, but by the "humane liberality of Tan Tock Seng, Esqr., J.P., Chinese Merchant of Singapore,"[22] and most of the support for this one hospital for the general public continued for some years to come from the Chinese community. It was not, however, until the latter part of the century that even elementary legislation with respect to contagious diseases was invoked, and serious governmental efforts to deal with matters of public health, such as infant and maternal mortality,[23]

66

and the more common diseases and the medical programs of dealing with them, developed only after
the turn of the century.

Despite the insistence by Singapore's founder
that "education must keep pace with commerce in
order that its benefits may be ensured and its
evils avoided,"[24] the subsequent history of the
colony indicates that both the East India Company
and the British Colonial Office were inclined
toward a laissez faire policy with respect to both
trade and education. The one governmental support
of public education in Singapore was at a low level
throughout the nineteenth century and even the one
educational institution directly supported by the
state and founded by Raffles received only sporadic
and indifferent encouragement. The educational
policy of the government under the British during
the first hundred years of the colony may be summarized as follows:

> The Bengal Government at first was doubtful
> about the continuation of Singapore as a
> British possession. Trade, and the preser-
> vation thereof, was its chief anxiety. . . .
> When the Transfer to the Colonial Office
> was made in 1867, the new Government con-
> tinued the grants paid by the old. Of-
> ficial attention, however, was drawn to
> the far from satisfactory account of the
> present state of education in the Colony,
> and a Select Committee of the Legislative
> Council was appointed to inquire into the
> matter. On the 8th December 1870 they re-
> ported "that the progress of education had
> been slow and uncertain," partly owing to

the want of sufficient encouragement from
the Government. . . . In 1886 an official
comment is that "not a single teacher now
remains who was a teacher in any of the
Singapore schools five years." They could
get larger wages as policemen or peons. . . .
Parsimony and indifference go hand in
hand. . . . In the two years before the War
(1912 and 1913) the amount voted for education was less than 3 per cent of the reve-
nue actually obtained in the Colony.[25]

The failure of the government to assume any major

initiative in public education led to the practice,

which has persisted markedly down to the present,

of religious and racial organizations establishing

and conducting their own schools, with such finan-

cial subsidy as they could derive from the state.

A further consequence of the permissive policy

of the government with respect to education has

been the perpetuation of sharply differentiated

language systems and modes of life-organization

within the community. Within ten years of the

founding of the colony there were a half dozen pri-

vately supported schools teaching in their separate

languages and lifestyles--"the parrot-like repeti-

tion of the Koran" in the Malay schools, mentioned

by Raffles, and probably the equally mechanical

memorization of the Chinese classics in the one

Hokkien and the two Cantonese schools, in addition

to the highly disciplined missionary and English-

speaking schools. A few years later instruction

in Tamil was begun at another school, and within

68

twenty years of the city's founding, children were being taught, chiefly in privately operated schools, in six different languages or dialects--English, Malay, Tamil, Cantonese, Hokkien, and Teochew.

The acceptance by the government and the persistence during the entire colonial period of separate schools with distinctive means of communication and varied curricula have obviously figured prominently in the survival of discrete cultures and communities until today, and it is highly probable that a central element in the national ideology of the postcolonial era, namely multiracialism, has been largely sustained from this long-continued practice. The government-supported schools growing directly out of Raffles' interest in education originally contained English, Chinese, and Malay classes, but the Malay department was abolished in 1842 owing to "the great apathy and even prejudice which exists among this race against receiving instruction."[26] The separate dialects taught in the schools supported by the Chinese during most of the nineteenth century gradually gave place to the exclusive use of Mandarin in the twentieth century, as the Chinese nationalist movement gained strength and the pressures from outside forced upon all Chinese, regardless of their dialectal origins, a sense of their common culture and regard in the eyes

69

of outsiders. Toward the close of the colonial period, four separate "language streams" had e-merged--English, Chinese (Mandarin), Malay, and Tamil--as permanent and fully accepted aspects of the public educational plan. English, as the language of the administering power was favored in both government and mission schools and some students from all racial groups found it advantageous to attend schools conducted in the English language, whereas the Chinese, Malay, and Tamil schools were attended mainly, if not exclusively, by persons from these respective groups. It was further observed, however, that:

> The British administrators, while allowing the situation to perpetuate itself, in fact favoured the English and Malay language streams, and in particular appeared to discriminate against the Chinese. But the latter, through the generous support of their own people, and in spite of severe handicaps were able to grow in strength and stature so that even as late as 1952, the Chinese school enrolment (74,104) exceeded that of all the other language streams combined (Malay 8,579; English 63,386; Tamil 1,205; total 73,170).[27]

British preeminence in the political and economic realms of Singapore during the colonial period (up to December 1941) is, of course, universally recognized, especially in the light of their limited numbers in the population. Throughout this entire period, the British occupied the positions of final political authority as the

70

Residents, Governors, Resident Councillors, Colonial
Secretaries, and prominent members of the Civil
Service.[28] So also in the judicial and legislative
branches of the government, British names predom-
inate, with an occasional non-Caucasian person as
an unofficial member of the Council or as a subordinate member of the judiciary--a justice of the
peace, perhaps. Certainly there was a great deal
of attention given by the administration to matters
thought to be for the welfare of the politically
subordinate but many times larger populations of
Malays, Chinese, Indians, and others who constituted the bulk of Singapore's inhabitants.

Despite the operation of the principle of
free trade by which the poorest immigrant from the
Orient theoretically enjoyed the same opportunity
to participate in the benefits of the marketplace
with the wealthiest and most influential member of
British aristocracy, the fact nevertheless remains
that the largest concentrations of economic power
had evolved into the hands of British individuals
or corporations during the colonial period. A
contemporary spokesman rationalizes this trend in
colonial society as follows:

> Singapore's history is essentially a part
> of that of Southeast Asia, the Far East,
> the British Empire and Britain itself.
> Singapore necessarily stands in acute
> relationship to the rest of the world, and

71

even today the critical digit in the relationship is the merchant, the adventurer in
commerce (albeit disguised in subfusc suiting),
the entrepeneur, substituting the goad of
profit (or the fear of failure) for the
rational impetus of mere utility. . . . The
true history of Singapore is to be found in
the annals of the merchant houses. . . .
If the government provided the roads, the
railways, and the harbours, it was the merchant houses which raised the capital in the
West for the great estates, the mines and the
tin-dredges, the godowns and the ships, the
oil storage depots and the financial sinews
of commerce. The role was as crucial as the
official role, and indeed continues to be--
for in the final analysis, commerce calls
the shots; a government of Singapore without
commerce, without industry, ceases to exist.
Only the deluge follows. And the commerce
of Singapore was primarily British commerce,
organized and brought to fruition by the
British Houses of Agency.[29]

More critically inclined observers, both within and

outside Singapore, have naturally been inclined to

interpret such developments as the evidence of

governmental favoritism and exploitation and the

valid grounds for no longer accepting British

colonial rule.

British recognition of the economic and

political advantage derived from their control over

Singapore led naturally to the efforts to protect

it militarily, and the peculiar merit of the island

as a center of trade for the entire region made it

also strategically useful as a stronghold to ensure

Britain's political dominance elsewhere in South-

east Asia. Investments of money and men, the

latter from various parts of the British Empire,

72

continued at a somewhat uneven pace to support
Singapore as a fortress from the days of Raffles
down to the present, but it cannot be said that
the military record of the colony under the
British was particularly brilliant. Most of the
military personnel had been recruited from else-
where--chiefly India and the United Kingdom--for
limited periods of time, and like all other tran-
sients in the community, there was little to
encourage rapport and close association with the
great mass of the resident population. Although
local volunteers were recruited, notably from
among the British and other Europeans and to a
lesser degree from among the Eurasians and the
other racial groups, but except for times of
emergency, the enthusiasm for the military was
apparently never very high.

Power Policies under Independence

The humiliating circumstances leading to the abject
surrender of Singapore to the Japanese on 15 Feb-
ruary 1942 witnessed not only the fall of the
supposed "Gibraltar of the East," but also the
demise of British colonial power in this part of
the world. During the war years 1942 to 1945
British prestige was of course at its lowest ebb,
not only because of the devastating military defeats
but also as a consequence of the growing resentment

73

on the part of the masses toward the system, in which the British and other Westerners seemed to have arrogated to themselves the rights and privileges of a master race. The return of the British military forces on 5 September 1945 was, however, scarcely more than a gesture of Britain's former political authority in Southeast Asia. Although Singapore continued as a Crown Colony until June 1959, there was little doubt that British rule was on its way out in Malaya, and the crucial question was how that change would occur and what new type of political control would take its place. As the young Chinese student from Singapore, then studying law at Cambridge University and later to become Prime Minister, stated in a speech in 1950:

> We in Malaya are now seeing British domination, after over a hundred years, enter its last phase. Colonial imperialism in Southeast Asia is dead except in Malaya, and our generation will see it out.

Regarding the sort of political and social structure he desired to see emerge, Lee Kuan Yew went on to say:

> But it is abundantly clear to Malayan vested interests, and that would include Chinese and Indian commercial interests, the Malay royal families, and the professional classes, that with the disappearance of the British Raj must also disappear the great inequality in wealth of the peoples of Malaya. For any independent Malayan government to exist, it must win popular support, and to gain any popular support it must promise, and do, social justice. . . . The

> first problem we face is that of racial
> harmony between Chinese and Malays. The
> second is the development of a united
> political front that will be strong e-
> nough, without resorting to armed force,
> to demand a transfer of power.[30]

The struggle to gain political independence and

to build a separate state in Singapore was much

too involved to permit detailed consideration here.

For present purposes, it may be sufficient to in-

dicate a few summary propositions, of which perhaps

the most obvious and fundamental relates to the

role which race has played and will no doubt con-

tinue to play.

Unquestionably the heavy predominance of Chi-

nese in the island's population (75 to 80 percent)

was a major factor in the decision to keep Singa-

pore as a separate political entity from the rest

of Malaya and thus avoid disturbing the delicate

balance of the races (slightly weighted toward

the Malays) which existed on the peninsula. How

sensitive these relationships might become and how

profoundly they might affect both the internal and

external stability of both Singapore and Malaysia

has been revealed again and again in confrontations

across racial lines--the protracted and vicious

warfare between Chinese Communists and persons of

all racial groups opposed to them, the Chinese-

Malayan-Indonesian confrontations and riots of

1964, and the Malay-Chinese-Indian conflagrations of May 1969, to mention only the more serious ones.

A growing awareness of how serious a threat to the welfare and solidarity of any community such internal divisiveness might become is reflected in the firm rejection by Singapore's chief minister and his government after Independence of race as a basis of political organization. While recognizing the incontestable fact of deep-seated and persistent cleavages across racial lines--differences in language and cultural values which seemed to dictate multiracialism as a cornerstone of the state for the indefinite future--there has been at least an official insistence on equal rights and treatment by the government for all persons regardless of race.

Singapore's present-day multiracialism combines recognition of the need for tolerance and appreciation of others across racial barriers, along with its acceptance of the legitimacy of separate languages and cultures, as reflected, for example, in the four official languages specified in the Constitution--Malay, English, Mandarin, and Tamil. This, at least, is the administrative policy, although the actual practice of these two somewhat antithetical principles obviously falls short of the profession. One spokesman for the administration presents the problem in the following terms:

> Already we are a multi-racial society and
> we are merely working out the logic of our
> character and general way of life. Ours is
> a policy of changing a multi-racial policy
> based on the separation of inward-looking
> groups into a pattern based on the coopera-
> tion of outward-looking groups. . . . Multi-
> racialism is part of our tradition. We accept
> each other--perhaps not fully in terms of co-
> operation but certainly not in terms of hos-
> tility. We are not seeking to kill racial
> hostility; we are out to stimulate to fuller
> meaning the existing racial cooperation.[31]

The government of Singapore, as an independent
nation since 1965, has thus far been able to deal
reasonably effectively with the internal problems
of maintaining peace and tolerance among the diverse racial groups within its borders--problems
which still plague the governments of many of the
countries of Southeast Asia. Drastic police methods, which appear to contravene the parliamentary
and democratic principles also espoused by the
Singapore government, have sometimes been invoked to
deal with emergency situations, such as the 13 May
1969 incident when it seemed possible that the violent racial tensions between Malays and Chinese
in Malaysia might spill across the border.

The aspects of race relations over which
Singapore has far less control still persist in
her associations with neighboring states and nations. Certainly this was a central issue underlying the long delay in working out a satisfactory

political relationship with Malaya, an objective
which is also recognized as highly important to
Singapore. The differing definitions within the
two states on the issue of what constitutes justice
in a multiracial community figured prominently in
the collapse in 1965 of the two-year experiment of
a political merger between them. The principles
incorporated in the Malayan Constitution of providing Malays with special rights and privileges to
governmental services and educational assistance
(supposedly in exchange for the advantages which
non-Malayans had been able to gain for themselves
in the economic realm) was not acceptable to the
dominant voting elements in Singapore. The efforts
of Singaporeans, notably Lee Kuan Yew, to urge a
"Malaysian Malaysia," in which equal rights would
be accorded to all persons on the basis of their
citizenship without regard to race or religion,
were defined by the dominant authorities in Malaya
as attempts to undermine the constitution and led
directly to the expulsion of Singapore as part of
the new nation. Despite the sharp differences on
racial policies which separate Singapore and Malaysia, the close economic interdependence of the two
nations has continued to be recognized and numerous
administrative links, such as a common system of
currency and of air transportation, continue to be
78

maintained.

A second principle or goal operating in Singapore's present political structure--probably no less important but just as difficult to define in operational terms as "multiracialism"--has been designated as "non-Communist, democratic socialism." Actually this ideal or combination of ideals grew out of the experience of Malaya and some of its young intellectuals at the close of World War II. The independence movement from Britain and toward Malayan nationalism received much of its impetus from British-educated Chinese and Malays who had been inoculated with the strong social-reform sentiments prevalent in England at that time. In the widely quoted speech in London to his fellow students from Malaya, urging them to accept leadership in the coming struggle for Independence, Lee Kuan Yew outlined in 1950 his major objectives, some of which were subsequently incorporated as the professed goals of the Republic of Singapore. These included, among others, "a moving faith in the practicability of a multi-racial society; an unmistakable rejection of communism; . . . and a clear commitment to the philosophy of socialism, to fairer shares for all, to a concern for the common man, provided that it is understood that nothing can be done for the common man without the intervention of

ruthless leadership--which he would provide."[32]   The
"fantastic discrepancies in wealth and power" inherent in colonialism, he claimed, were destined to
end whether the students took their part in the
movement or not, but he sought to impress upon the
intellectual elite their moral duty of leadership
in hastening and organizing the shift toward greater
equality in wealth among the peoples of Malaya.

Just how fantastic the discrepancies in wealth
and power were in Malaya and the degree to which
they were inherent in British colonialism depends
largely, of course, upon the perspective from which
these questions are approached. From the point of
view of the indoctrinated communists, the mere fact
that the European invaders had contributed merely of
their directing power over the Asian workers in the
economic development of Southeast Asia was reason
enough to undertake the mission of throwing off the
"exploiting parasites" by whatever means that were
available. The large masses of residents who had
become fully conscious of the contrast in the levels
of living between themselves and their European or
Chinese employers could not fail to be influenced
somewhat by the communist logic or the ruthless
dedication to which they pursued it. The bitter
and bloody campaign by the communist invaders
against the British military forces prior to 1959

80

and against the Malayan forces since then has necessarily had a profound impact upon the civilian communities, including Singapore, with sentiments and loyalties building up on both sides of the communist issue.

Like most politically defined goals, there has been considerable shifting in the meanings attached to the phrase "noncommunist, democratic socialism," even within the limited period of its major prominence in the campaign speeches of political candidates and in the attention of the general public. There were times in the late 1950s and early 60s, for example, when the People's Action party (P.A.P.) and its leaders were assumed by many, especially the British, to be in reality procommunist because of the presence in their ranks of persons outspokenly opposed to the professed party policy of noncommunism. Although there are aspects of the P.A.P. structure which are strongly suggestive of the communist pattern of organization, and although economic relations have been maintained with both Communist China and the U.S.S.R., it is quite clear that Singapore's major identifications and interactions have continued to be with the noncommunist West.

The idealism of "democratic socialism," as conceived by the leadership of Singapore's P.A.P.,

is perhaps best expressed in the language of the
Prime Minister who explained that his ideal society
was where "wealth and rank are not the arbiter of
a man's family fortune and the fate of his children, . . . where differences of language, religion
or culture are completely subdued by the identity of
common interests, in an equal and just society where
man is rewarded on the basis of merit and effort."[33]
The Prime Minister and his followers, however, found
themselves confronted with a capitalistic economy
which they "could not convert into a socialist
economy without disastrous consequences to everyone." The impossibility of achieving their ideal
in the face of the stark realities confronting
them in a competitive capitalist world led the
administration to seek a redistribution of wealth
and opportunity through the familiar devices of the
welfare state, without abandoning "the purity of
its ultimate beliefs." In this respect the Prime
Minister insisted that "democratic socialists could
be proud of having worked the capitalist system
efficiently."[34] This does not mean, however, that
communist sympathies and ideologies have ceased to
exist or appeal to the people of Singapore, but
under the provisions of the present administration
there is neither the disposition nor the effective
basis for expressing such sentiments among any large

portion of the population.

Notes

1. The term _race,_ as used in this study, follows
   the commonplace practice of identifying it
   with any group of "people who, because of
   commonly recognized external traits thought
   to be biologically inherited, have become self-
   conscious and are subject to differential
   treatment." The term _ethnic group,_ on the
   other hand, refers to a collection of people
   who are distinguished from others on the basis
   of shared cultural traits, such as language,
   dress, religious practices, or eating habits,
   regardless of any imputed biological characteristics. Since race, so conceived, is purely
   a matter of social discovery and usage, whereas
   the ethnic group can be objectively identified
   from verifiable criteria, these two terms may
   or may not coincide. A race may actually in-
   clude a number of different ethnic groups of
   whose existence outsiders are unaware.

2. Song Ong Siang, _op. cit._, p. 12.

3. Quoted by Purcell, _op. cit._, p. 73.

4. This phenomenon illustrates a significant
   principle of human interaction in the modern
   world, namely, that the conception of race
   commonly originates and continues to function
   chiefly as a human device for classifying or
   differentiating among the great mass of people
   who do not belong to one's own social world.
   "Race" functions, therefore, as an instrument
   for keeping all those outside one's own group
   at a certain social distance and for justify-
   ing the failure to establish further contact
   with them. The disposition to use the term
   ethnic group, or even to recognize the Chinese
   from Amoy as a distinct type among the out-
   group, reflects the beginning of communication
   with the outsiders and the breakdown of racial
   exclusiveness.

5. Song Ong Siang, _op. cit._, p. 25.

6. Other serious outbreaks of tension between
   groups within the Chinese community, involving
   chiefly Teochews and Hokkiens, occurred in

1871, 1872, and 1906. These are described
briefly by Song Ong Siang, op. cit., pp. 166,
402-404. There have also been many other
expressions of resentment by elements within
the Chinese community toward the British
authorities, the police, or other racial
groups, growing out of cultural conflicts and
misunderstandings of various sorts, but these
are not the problems with which we are concerned at this point.

7. If the figures given in Table 2 for the
    Straits-born had been allocated to the dia-
    lectal groups from which these persons were
    descended, the proportion of Hokkiens in 1891
    would probably have been well over 40 percent,
    possibly as high as 44 percent, and the per-
    centages of Teochews and Cantonese would also
    have been somewhat higher.

8. M. V. Del Tufo, A Report on the 1947 Census of
    Population (London, 1949), p. 76.

9. C. A. Vlieland, A Report on the 1931 Census and
    on Certain Problems of Vital Statistics (Lon-
    don, 1932), p. 84.

10. Sinnappah Arasaratnam, Indians in Malaysia and
    Singapore (Bombay, 1970), p. 35.

11. Charles Burton Buckley, An Anecdotal History
    of Old Times in Singapore (Kuala Lumpur, 1965),
    p. 61.

12. George Windsor Earl, The Eastern Seas in 1832-
    34 as quoted in Donald and Joanna Moore, The
    First 150 Years of Singapore (Singapore, 1969),
    p. 170.

13. Hayes Marriott, "The Peoples of Singapore,"
    in Walter Makepeace, One Hundred Years of
    Singapore (London, 1921), pp. 356-357

14. M. V. Del Tufo, op. cit., p. 72.

15. C. A. Vlieland, op. cit., p. 75.

16. C. A. Vlieland, op. cit., p. 87.

17. M. V. Del Tufo, op cit., p. 18.

18. K. G. Tregonning, Malaysia and Singapore
    (Singapore, 1967).

84

19. <u>Ibid</u>., pp. 18, 23.

20. Sir Richard Winstedt, <u>The</u> <u>Malays:</u> <u>A</u> <u>Cultural</u> <u>History</u> (London, 1961), pp. 176-178.

21. Dr. Gilbert E. Brooke, "Medical Work and Institutions," in Walter Makepeace (editor), <u>One</u> <u>Hundred</u> <u>Years</u> <u>of</u> <u>Singapore</u> (London, 1921), pp. 487-495.

22. Song Ong Siang, <u>op</u>. <u>cit</u>., p. 63.

23. According to Dr. Brooke, as late as 1911 somewhat more than one-third (345.5 per 1,000) of all infants born to mothers in Singapore that year died during the same year. This compared with a rate of 106 per thousand in 1910 for England and Wales. By the year 1917 the infant mortality rate had dropped to somewhat less than a third, but it varied markedly among Singapore's racial groups as follows: Europeans, 93.2 per 1,000; Chinese, 294; Malays, 432.6; and Indian, 206.5.

24. Part of statement by Sir Stamford Raffles to leading inhabitants of Singapore on the 1st April, 1823, and quoted by C. Bazell, "Education in Singapore," in Walter Makepeace, <u>op</u>. <u>cit</u>., p. 427.

25. C. Bazell, <u>op</u>. <u>cit</u>., pp. 461-465.

26. <u>Ibid</u>., p. 435.

27. Gwee Yee Hean, "Education and the Multi-Racial Society," in Ooi Jin-Bee and Chiang Hai Ding (editors), <u>Modern</u> <u>Singapore</u> (Singapore, 1969), p. 209.

28. "Executive government was in the hand of the Malayan Civil Service, recruited mainly in Britain from 'natural born British subjects of pure European descent on both sides.' Subordinate posts were covered by a Straits Civil Service, open to British subjects of all races. The senior government officials worked in consultation with the leading European non-officials and with a section of the small group of wealthy and professional Asians."-- C. M. Turnbull, "Constitutional Development, 1819-1968," in Ooi Jin-Bee, <u>op</u>. <u>cit</u>., p. 184.

29. Donald and Joanna Moore, <u>op</u>. <u>cit</u>., p. 482.

30. Donald and Joanna Moore, op. cit., pp. 670-671.

31. George C. Thomson, "Problems of Race in a Multi-Racial Society," in Singapore: The Way Ahead (Singapore, 1967), p. 18.

32. Donald and Joanna Moore, op. cit., p. 673.

33. Quoted in Alex Josey, Lee Kuan Yew (Singapore, 1968), p. 58.

34. Ibid.

3

A CHINESE UNIVERSITY IN A FOREIGN SETTING

Schools for the nurturing of their children are among the first of the institutions which immigrants to foreign lands seek to have established for themselves, once they have become reconciled to a more or less permanent residence in the adopted country. There is a well-nigh universal assumption on the part of immigrant parents that their children should at least be able to communicate freely in the mother tongue and to accept the basic moral values of the homeland, but the satisfaction of these concerns rarely requires the establishment of schools much beyond the elementary level or the type of schooling to which the parents were accustomed in their native village. Immigrants of peasant origin may, in fact, look upon formal education beyond the traditional level as a potential threat to their way of life and especially as endangering the economic ambitions which were the foremost factors in bringing them to the new land.

The founding by the Nanyang Chinese of an educational institution with objectives far beyond those of the village school or even the secondary or trade school was, therefore, something quite extra-

ordinary.[1] There is probably no other institution
of higher learning in any part of the world comparable to Nanyang University in having been developed out of the concerns and efforts of an immigrant labor group for the advanced education of
their youth. A major function of this chapter
will be, therefore, to sort out and examine some
of the major influences which led to the creation
and development of this institution.

The two obvious sets of forces which mold the
character of any immigrant institution are those
brought from the homeland and those derived from
the adopted land, although in reality it is difficult to disentangle the two, and virtually impossible to measure their relative strength or influence upon each other. Special interest naturally
centers upon the extra pressures within the Chinese
community in Singapore which brought forth this
unique institution, but first it is necessary to
examine somewhat more closely the nature of the
Chinese community itself, particularly as it relates
to education.

Shifting Pressures within the Chinese Community
Throughout the history of the Chinese community in
Singapore there have been elements in the situation
which would militate against the development of educational interests of any sort, much less of a

88

university of their own. An example is the fact that throughout the first hundred years of its existence, the Chinese community consisted overwhelmingly of men. This prevented the formation of normal family life and the bearing of children for whom schools might be needed. As recently as 1921 there were still more than twice as many males as females, and even after the close of World War II (1947) there was still a significant excess (17.9 percent) of males over females in the adult population. A strikingly high ratio of adults prevailed among the Chinese until after the 1931 Census, when 64 percent were twenty years of age or over, and this also served to discourage any great amount of interest in education, or at least higher education. Within thirty years, these particular abnormalities had largely disappeared, but another, likely to have at least a temporary depressing effect upon Chinese interest in higher education, had taken its place. This was the sudden spurt in the infant and child population, such that by 1957 somewhat less than half (43.8 percent) of the Chinese had not yet reached the age of fifteen years, and the educational concerns for them were more likely to be centered at the primary and secondary levels.

Prior to World War II, the Chinese population

of Singapore had consisted predominantly of first-generation immigrants, and it could hardly be expected that a people with its language and early memories largely rooted in another country would have been able to develop enthusiasm for an institution of higher learning in the new land, even if it were designed to perpetuate the values of the homeland. In 1921, only 25.1 percent of the Chinese in the colony had been born in Malaya, and ten years later this ratio was still only 35.6 percent. Primarily as a consequence of the legal restrictions on further immigration imposed in 1932 and 1938 following the worldwide depression, the proportion of immigrants in Singapore's Chinese population declined greatly, and shortly after the close of the war, well over half (59.9 percent) of the Chinese residents had been born in Malaya, predominantly in the city itself. By 1957 nearly three-quarters (73.2 percent) of Singapore's Chinese had been born within Malaya, and this figure reached 82.2 percent according to the 1966 survey.

Still other factors likely to have a retarding effect upon any disposition among the Chinese to build a university of their own can be readily recognized, if not so easily reflected in statistical terms. The origin of Singapore's Chinese from among the impoverished, dispossessed, and largely

illiterate peasantry of South China does not suggest
a promising source from which to secure large sums
of money for an institution of higher learning.
The village background in China, like that of most
of the peasant emigrants from other parts of the
world, was not such as to develop initially any
great appreciation for university sophistication.

> The emigrants were poor peasants or
> labourers and knew little of the fine art
> and literature of classical China. . . .
> They brought peasant habits and a peasant
> outlook, as did many an Italian or Greek
> or Levantine who emigrated, for the same
> reasons, to the United States of America.[2]

The cultural dispositions which the Chinese emigrants brought with them were necessarily more
centrally directed to satisfying the elementary
needs of food, clothing, and shelter for themselves, their children, and their kinfolk, whether
overseas or in China. Such basic concerns were
foremost in the minds of virtually all of the new
arrivals during the early period of their residence
overseas, and they have continued to occupy such
a central place for them except as they have succeeded in moving up the economic ladder.

On the other side of the ledger, it must be
recognized that there were special elements in
the Chinese heritage and particularly in the
peculiar circumstances of the Chinese residents in
Malaya and Singapore which encouraged the founding

of such an institution as Nanyang University. Although the pattern of life in most overseas communities tends to reenforce Raffles' early judgment that the merchants constituted "the higher and more respectable class" among the Chinese in Singapore and that they therefore deserved special consideration in their assignment to sites within the community, this "does not accord with the traditional Chinese order of the classes which places the scholar first."[3] Respect for knowledge, amounting actually to reverence, was so central in the traditional Chinese pattern of life that even the lowliest peasant unconsciously recognized the exalted place of the sage or scholar, even though he, the peasant, had little or no understanding of what this knowledge consisted. The highest ideal of Confucian ethics, so Chinese philosophers claimed, was to educate men to be sages.[4] Moreover, since political advancement in the old Chinese order had always rested on scholastic achievement, measured by performance in public examination open to all, the successful candidate was the boast and pride of his village. Lin Yutang, the first but not too successful president of Nanyang University, went so far as to identify the whole of China "as a land where scholars are the ruling class, and in times of peace, at least, the worship of scholar-

92

ship has always been sedulously cultivated."[5]

This respect for scholarship explains in large part the widespread practice noted in all overseas Chinese communities of setting up schools as soon as their children were old enough to attend them. The curriculum in most of these schools, at least in their early stages, consisted almost exclusively of the memorization of Chinese characters and of portions of the classics, and scholarly regard was commonly expressed in the mechanical repetition of words of the sages without very much concern for what they might mean either to the individual or to society. In other words, the respect for scholarship, when it becomes a form of worship and is supported by age-old traditions of sanctity, may degenerate into scholasticism, and this, of course, has continued to be the major limitation in traditional Chinese education as it has been perpetuated in the overseas areas, including Malaya. Although the classics continued to receive dominant emphasis in the schools conducted by the Chinese in Singapore during most of the nineteenth century and extending well into the twentieth century, additional stress was beginning to be placed upon them as a means of "ennobling man's mind and of purifying his character."[6] Insofar as this actually occurred, the Chinese schools could provide a suitable foundation on which to build a Chinese university.

Certainly the traditional concern for scholarship does figure prominently in the support which the Chinese community of Singapore has given to their own primary and secondary schools down to the present, although it is also contended that as late as the 1950s, "only a small percentage of Chinese students enter secondary schools, and fewer acquire a university education."[7] The British policy throughout the colonial period of encouraging the native and immigrant labor groups to assume the responsibility for the education of their own children, "under their own teachers, in their own language"--subsidized financially, perhaps from government sources--meant that most Chinese resources and enthusiasm for education were necessarily directed toward their primary and secondary schools. Even after the adoption of the principle of free primary education in any one of the four recognized languages, the British administrators "favoured the English and Malay language streams, and in particular appeared to discriminate against the Chinese."[8] In spite of such official discrimination, Chinese concern for the perpetuation of their own language was such that as late as 1952 the Chinese school enrollment continued to exceed that of all the other language streams combined.[9]

94

Pride in the ancestral culture has been another closely related factor reenforcing the disposition among the Chinese community to establish their own schools--first at the elementary level, later for secondary students, and finally a university of their own. The sense on the part of the Chinese--even the most illiterate and impoverished--that they belong to an ancient and honored lineage encourages not only an emphasis upon the importance of preserving that heritage, but also on the value of keeping it pure and undefiled from outside influences. In order to survive in any organized sense, every racial or ethnic group must have developed some feeling of pride in itself--its customs, values, and history--and people with a long and widely recognized civilization, such as the Chinese, naturally are highly conscious of their inheritance and consequently may regard with disdain people who seem, from their perspective, to be less adequately endowed. Even among the relatively high proportion of Chinese engaged in occupations affording low incomes and prestige throughout Singapore's history, a confidence has persisted that they are the bearers of a worthy tradition which other peoples do not possess. To many outsiders, such apparent logical blindness must reflect a deeply imbedded cultural arrogance, and even con-

95

temporary historians feel justified to characterize it as follows:

> The /Chinese/ culture is so strong, so
> deep, so uniquely exclusive, as to be
> virtually impenetrable . . . . This
> characteristic was perpetuated undiluted
> in the Chinese schools--thus compounding
> and confirming Chinese separateness. No
> one could share in their culture, and
> they, steeped in their own, isolated by
> its language and script and overwhelmed
> by its chauvinistic irrelevance, were un-
> able to participate in anyone else's . . . .
> It is for this reason that even today on
> Boat Quay, in the very heart of Singapore,
> where the first godowns were built in
> Raffles' day, there are businesses as
> unbreakably, unalterably Chinese as if they
> had never left China. Embedded within a
> swirling confluence of cultures, in the
> fourth largest port of the world, they
> have remained untouched by anyone's in-
> fluence but their own!10

So also the refusal of Chinese school authorities to accept full grants-in-aid from the government in 1954 seemed to imply a fear of outside, therefore inferior, and certainly less acceptable control over the education of their children.

Immigrant Relations to the Homeland

Owing to a variety of factors the Chinese emigrants to Southeast Asia were virtually state orphans. Although such earlier dynasties of China as the Ming (1368-1644) and the Ch'ing (1644-1911) had vigorously discouraged emigration even under the threat of beheading, it was especially under the Manchus that persons from Fukien and Kwangtung who managed to escape to Nanyang came to be regarded as poten-

96

tial traitors plotting to overthrow the government. Opposition to the Manchu conquerors had been strongest and most persistent in the provinces of South China, and it was assumed that those who sought to leave the country were the most dangerous of the conspirators.

Hence, the government of China under the Manchus made no effort to look after the welfare of those who were insolent enough to leave the benefits of the Middle Kingdom, and it was, of course, in the emigrant colonies of the Nanyang and elsewhere that the revolutionary movements, leading to the overthrow of the Manchu government in 1911, drew their strongest support, both moral and financial.

Singapore's Chinese community was notable as "a rendezvous for political refugees from China, prominent among whom were Sun Yat-sen, Wang Ching-wei, and Hu Han-min."[11] It was only natural, therefore, that the government resulting from the 1911 revolution should reflect its appreciation for the assistance received from its emigrants by reversing the Manchu policy and instead dealing with them as loyal citizens of China, to be protected abroad and to be welcomed at home for their financial support and as visitors or residents whenever they chose to return. One of the consequences of this changed policy of the government in China was to encourage the Nanyang Chinese, insofar as their circumstances would permit, to send their children back to the ancestral communities for their education. This also applied in a more limited degree to education at the university level as interest developed overseas in the cultivation of traditional scholarship.

The spread, both before and after the 1917 Russian revolution, of Marxist and communist ideology into China and its subsequent diffusion in the communities overseas dampened considerably the enthusiasm of the British government in Malaya toward the free movement of migrants between the two countries, particularly of communist-indoctrinated returnees as teachers. The Japanese occupation afforded an especially convenient occasion for infiltrating Malaysia with ideas and guerilla forces directed against the colonialists, both Japanese and British. There was enough of a sense of their having been exploited and discriminated against among the immigrants to Malaya to provide the communist invaders with a substantial group of sympathizers, even among the Chinese in Singapore. The rapid expansion of communist control on the mainland of China and the rising influence of the People's Republic of China as one of the major world powers after 1950 opened the way for the unprece-

98

dented development among the overseas Chinese of
a sense of their kinship with a nation of prime
stature. Even among the great majority of the
Chinese immigrants and their children whose primary
orientations and basic values were distinctly non-
communist, the emergence of China as a first-rate
power inevitably stirred some feelings of pride and
wonder, no matter how far removed from the ancestral
land by generation or cultural sympathies the individual might be.

The long (1948-1960) and bitter struggle of
the British, supported by the Malayans, to drive the
communist guerillas out of the country, left a
residue of distaste within the independent governments of both Malaysia and Singapore toward Communist China which made it difficult, although by
no means impossible, for the children and youth
of the Chinese in the region to continue to be sent
back to the ancestral homeland for their further
education.

The Founding of Nanyang University

The presence and interaction of the various factors discussed thus far in this chapter underlie
the bold venture, formally undertaken in May 1953,
"to promote a university where the Chinese language
would be used as the chief medium of instruction.[12]
Without undertaking research beyond the scope of

99

this study, it would be impossible to state with any precision the degree to which each has operated, but certainly a combination of these and possibly other influences had been at work. The statement on the history of the institution, appearing in the official calendar refers directly only to certain of the forces we have discussed, but others are included at least by inference.

> In the colonial days before World War II,
> Chinese education in the region now com-
> prising the Federation of Malaysia and
> the Republic of Singapore was virtually
> the sole responsibility of the resident
> Chinese community itself rather than the
> concern of the colonial government. As
> might be expected, their school system
> followed closely the pattern prevailing
> in China. Although this development
> of Chinese education before the War did
> not proceed beyond the secondary stage,
> there was no difficulty for students
> coming out of the Chinese high schools
> to return to their home-land for higher
> education. That was precisely what they
> used to do until China came under Com-
> munist rule in 1949, which brought an
> abrupt halt to the flow of Chinese high-
> school graduates seeking higher educa-
> tion in China.
>
> The colonial government which had hitherto
> shunned responsibility for Chinese edu-
> cation did not seem to appreciate the
> magnitude and seriousness of this problem
> precipitated by the closing of the avenue
> for higher education to numerous Chinese
> high-school leavers, for they continued
> to keep these young people out of bounds
> to the then budding University of Malaya,
> the government supported only institution
> of higher education serving this region.13

Many of the political analyses of Singapore during the critical days before and after indepen-

100

dence, including a government white paper published in Kuala Lumpur in 1964, give a different interpretation of the founding and early history of the university. The founders are represented in some accounts as staunch Chinese racialists who had become the unwitting pawns of the newly established People's Republic of China. It was conceded that much of the impetus for the founding of Nanyang University had come from wealthy Chinese in Singapore and elsewhere in Malaya who were at the outset anything but sympathetic with the communist regime in China,[14] having been identified with the Kuomintang and the Nationalist government in Taiwan. The stormy experience of the early years of the institution seemed to indicate to these observers that communist influences must have been operating effectively behind the scenes.

It was even suggested that some of these business leaders, including Tan Lark Sye, the rich rubber merchant who became the first chairman of the university, had "either made extensive contributions as a kind of 'protection money' to the Communist operations all over Southeast Asia and/or appeared to be motivated by a combination of cultural pride and a conviction that Southeast Asia must sooner or later fall under People's China's hegemony."[15] The next step of referring to the university as "Communist-oriented," and "Com-munist-contrived," was easily made.[16] Lee Kuan Yew, on the other hand, according to his biographer Alex Josey, was apparently inclined to interpret the com-munist-supportive activities of Tan Lark Sye, for which he was deprived of his citizenship in 1964, "not because Tan was pro-communist, but because he was a Chinese chauvinist"--on the grounds that "out of extreme racialist sentiments he knowingly allowed himself to be used by his associates to advocate the communist cause in Malaya."[17]

The pronounced emphasis upon "Communists in the Nanyang University" in the Malaysian government white paper with that title in 1964 could be inter-preted in part as a means of publicizing the jeopar-dy to the Malaysian nation resulting from its in-clusion of Singapore. Without contending that the founders of Nanyang were themselves communists, the paper argues that the institution was a ready-made instrument for the communists to utilize for their own purposes.

> It was a strange coincidence for the
> Communists that 1956, the year which
> saw the crushing defeat of their open
> front organisations, also saw the first
> enrolment of students for the Nanyang
> University which was to provide them
> with a situation their Communist indoc-
> trinated followers knew well how to ex-
> ploit to their advantage. In Jurong
> Road old lessons were to be applied,
> new tactics developed, and new cadres

trained to put them into effect.[18]
Fear of possible communist domination undoubtedly
contributed significantly to the resistance in
government circles in Singapore to the announcement
in January 1953 that the Singapore Hokkien Hui Kuan
proposed raising funds for the establishment of a
Chinese university on the island, although the
basis for the opposition most commonly announced
was that such an institution would militate against
the "declared policy of the Government to create a
united Malayan nation."[19]

Nevertheless from within the Chinese communities throughout Southeast Asia, the response to the
idea of a university for the Nanyang Chinese appears
to have been considerable, judging by the large
amount of money raised, from cabdrivers and hawkers
to wealthy tycoons, and the gift of a 525-acre
campus on an abandoned rubber plantation located
15 miles from the center of Singapore. The initial
enthusiasm for this project was, of course, generated from a number of different sources. The belief,
expressed by Dato Sir Cheng-lock Tan, head of the
influential Malayan Chinese Association, that nearly
400,000 Chinese students in the Federation and
Singapore would have no opportunity to secure a
university education unless permitted to attend a
Chinese institution, was undoubtedly widely shared.

The fact that the overwhelming majority of the students of Chinese ancestry with a completed secondary education had received their instruction in Mandarin meant that they were not eligible to matriculation in the only existing university, where classes were held in the English language. Certainly pride in the ancestral culture and the concern for its preservation, as suggested earlier, were important considerations. Insofar as a desire to provide an effective base from which to disseminate communist propaganda among Chinese throughout the whole of Southeast Asia may have figured in the early support given to the movement for the new university--and there can be but little doubt that it did--this was assuredly only one factor interwoven with others.

The opposition of the British authorities, together with unsettled political conditions in Singapore, delayed the opening of the new institution until March 1956, still without official blessing. In the meantime there were other reverses. The first chancellor, the widely heralded and highly prestigious Lin Yu-tang, resigned in March 1955 after only a few months of service. The insistence on the part of the principal financial promoters, as a board of managers, on their right to determine the policies led to irreconcilable differences with the strong-willed chancellor, and a substitute

104

administration had therefore been established before the university could open its doors to its first group of students.

The state of social unrest in Singapore throughout the 1950s associated with the movement toward political independence was manifested among other ways in the disturbed conditions and the mass demonstrations in the Chinese middle schools, from which most of the Nanyang University students were drawn. The emotionally disturbed atmosphere in the Chinese educational circles in Singapore, in which the Nanyang students during the first decade of the university's history had been nurtured, is represented by the government white paper as follows:

> Through the text books in use in Singapore Chinese schools from the primary level upwards and in the teachers directly and recently arrived from the ideological turbulence which was twentieth century China, Chinese Middle School children in Singapore were encouraged to identify themselves politically with institutions and ideas of relevance in the context of China's internal affairs.
>
> The Communists of Singapore, following the Leninist precepts of agitation as the avenue to power, did not therefore have far to go in search of an issue with the greatest following, the greatest explosive power, and the greatest reserves of unused intellectual activity and effective leadership. Social frustration, cultural chauvinism, and racial appeal blended in mutual re-enforcement, while the Communist cadres by agitation, organization and manipulation directed these

forces towards the achievement of their Communist purposes, and to the damage of the group and the culture they claim to defend.[20]

Granting the rhetorical overstatement in passages such as this, the actual events of the day reveal an unquestionable linkage between the activities and announced policies of the officially recognized Malayan communist party and the demonstrations by students of the Chinese schools, initially at the secondary level and later among the students at Nanyang University. A series of violent demonstrations involving Chinese middle-high students, such as the May 13 incident of 1954, and the May 12, 1955 outburst "when riots, fomented by students from the Chinese schools, in support of a bus employees strike, tore the city apart, and two policemen, an American reporter and a student were killed and many were injured,"[21] were in a sense the precursors to the disturbances in which Nanyang University students were central participants a few years later.

The unsettled state of the Nanyang student body during the first decade of the university's history, to which most published references to the institution allude, was of course a consequence of numerous factors, of which communist infiltration was only one. Even the government white paper called attention to the university's vulnerability

106

to pressures from other than communist sources.

> The lack of planning, principle or tradi-
> tion and the anomalies of administration,
> the low morale of the staff with the per-
> petual Democles (sic) sword of a one-year
> contract and the consequential one-year im-
> migration permit hanging over their /fac-
> ulty/ head, laid the University wide open
> to the attacks of determined and dedicated
> Communist cadres and particularly, of those
> who had come through the experience of the
> Chinese Middle School troubles and agita-
> tions from 1948 to 1955. The appointment
> as Vice-Chancellor of a former Middle
> School Principal who had submitted to pre-
> vious Communist intimidation was the final
> act that brought the University student
> body under severe Communist influence.[22]

The account by an American political scientist pro-

vides a slightly different interpretation, but one

that is not inconsistent with the foregoing.

> . . . almost at once the university ran
> into problems of Chinese politics since
> it attracted both nationalists and Com-
> munists. The university has also had
> constant trouble with excessive control
> by its financial backers and by student
> agitators, threatening academic freedom.
> Student demonstrations have forced the
> government to send riot squads into the
> campus several times. Difficulty in
> getting first-rate staff has contributed
> to low standards and ultimately to prob-
> lems in placing students.[23]

The brief historical account in the official uni-

versity calendar mentions also the additional dif-

ficulty that although the university's status as

an institution of higher education in the country's

educational system was officially recognized by the

Singapore Legislative Assembly in March 1959, for

another eight years even the Singapore government

and its civil service refused to recognize the Nanyang degrees. Such public discrimination and the consequent lack of confidence in Nanyang graduates on the part of private employers quite naturally intensified still further the unrest within the institution between both students and faculty.

So great was the demand among Chinese throughout Southeast Asia for advanced education of their youth that the university continued to grow in the size of the student body and in financial support from the Chinese community. When the first students were enrolled in March 1956, they were distributed among eight departments--Chinese Language and Literature, Modern Language and Literature, History and Geography, Economics and Political Science, and Education in a College of Arts, and Mathematics, Physics, Chemistry and Biology in a College of Science. The following year a third College of Commerce was created with two departments of Industrial Management and of Accountancy and Banking, establishing a structural pattern which remained intact down to the present. Although only the first phase of the building program had been completed by the third year of the school's existence, the pressures of students seeking admission was greater than the limited facilities of the physical plant and of qualified faculty could properly accommodate.

108

The overly rapid expansion of the student body to
1,874 in 1961 and to 2,527 in 1963, with a faculty
of only 146, was an important factor leading to the
series of official investigations of the university,
culminating in the widely discussed and contro-
versial Report of the Wang Gungwu Review Committee
in 1965.

Governmental Concern with Nanyang

Public and official skepticism regarding the educational quality of Nanyang University and its
desirability as an institution dominated by Chinese
language and culture in a multiracial setting
continued, however, long after the 1959 passage of
the University Ordinance, granting governmental
authorization and status. Prime Minister Lee Kuan
Yew, in his address to the students and faculty on
28 October 1959, warned of the dangers inherent in
an exclusively communal approach to higher education
in the new institution, pointing out that despite
Singapore's predominantly Chinese population,
Southeast Asia was overwhelmingly Malaysian.

> You must appreciate that Nanyang Uni-
> versity can best succeed and flourish if
> it is accepted as a Malaysian university
> and not just a Singapore university. . . .
> Throughout the whole of Southeast Asia,
> where about fifteen million Chinese are
> scattered, they are being discriminated
> against because they are considered as
> having remained distinct and separate
> from the local communities, both in the
> use of their language and in the observ-

ance of the customs, habits, and culture . . . . Our geographical and eth-
nological positions are realities which
we must face. A resurgent China is already the object, not just of admiration,
but also of apprehension amongst the
peoples of Southeast Asia. And if Nanyang were to become symbolized as an
outpost in Southeast Asia of Chinese
dominance, then we will only have our-
selves to blame if we find the position
deepened and embittered.[24]

In an address to Nanyang students in March of the

following year, the Prime Minister was even more

direct and emphatic in his insistence that the

exclusive use at the university of an immigrant

language, such as Chinese, had politically explo-

sive potentialities. He went on to say that al-

though Chinese would continue to be the chief

medium of instruction at Nanyang for the immediate

future, "with every passing year more and more of

the national language /Malay/ must be taught and

used, to keep in line with the trend of Malaya's

linguistic future, and also to fit Nantah students

to play a useful role in Malayan society."[25]

Four years later, after the incorporation of

Singapore in the newly formed nation of Malaysia,

the government's concern regarding Nanyang had be-

come focused more directly upon the alleged com-

munist infiltration of the student body rather

than their preoccupation with the superiority of

Chinese language and culture, although the two were

110

obviously closely related. The government white
paper on communism in the Nanyang University, published in July 1964, does not at any point state
or even imply that the student body as a whole had
ever been procommunist in its loyalties or inclinations. It seeks rather to document the proposition that from the outset the control of the
Students' Union, departmental organizations, and
publications, as well as the Guild of Graduates,
had been seized and exploited for their own ul-
terior purposes by a procommunist minority. Without citing or attempting to evaluate the detailed
evidence presented in this report, data from this
and other sources indicate that a small but effectively organized and disciplined corps of students, graduates, and outsiders succeeded rather
well in maneuvering student associations in support
of communist objectives, such as opposition to the
merger of Singapore with the Federation of Malaya.[26]
The white paper summarized the state of this leadership in 1964 as follows:

> There is a clear continuity of policy,
> leadership, tactics and techniques in
> the activities of the Singapore Chi-
> nese Middle Schools Union to the Nan-
> yang University Students Union and on
> to the Guild of Nanyang University
> Graduates as the same group have moved
> forward along the Chinese language
> stream. They now oppose the National
> Government of Malaysia in the same
> strength and by the same methods as

111

they opposed the colonial government of Malaya.

> They have exploited the ineffective leadership and administrative defects of the Nanyang University and become the effective masters of its policy and administration, including appointments to, and the control of, the academic staff. For this purpose they have resisted any attempts at reform aimed at improving the academic stature of the University, and therefore of the degrees it confers.[27]

Governmental concern over what seemed like a rising tide of communist influence at Nanyang had become so acute by 1963 that, coincident with confrontation between Indonesia and Malaysia, the Singapore authorities took into custody several university students along with political and labor leaders on the ground that they were engaged in procommunist subversive activities. Later the same year, following the Merger and the elections, more student leaders at Nanyang and graduates were arrested, and rioting broke out on the campus between student sympathizers and the police, resulting in injuries to four students and a subsequent three-day boycott of classes. Continued unrest on the Nanyang campus, especially marked during the three years 1963 to 1965, during which Singapore was part of Malaysia, was certainly led by students with communist orientations, but it was also an expression of even stronger nurturing

112

agencies in the wider community, including the Barisan Sosialis and the communist underground. A vigorous campaign on the part of both the Singapore and the federal Malaysian authorities during the same period resulted in the previously mentioned loss of citizenship on the part of Tan Lark Sye, the strongest financial supporter of the university.

The growing realization on the part of the government of Singapore, after Independence, that Nanyang University, whatever its early limitations, possessed a great potential for the educational future of the country, led to efforts for genuine accommodation rather than merely of criticism or attack. The initial steps, beginning in January 1959 with the setting up of a governmental commission "to look into the academic standards of Nanyang University and the adequacy of the teaching staff and the equipment, and of the means adopted by Nanyang University for ensuring satisfactory standards of academic work," arrived in less than a month at conclusions that were scarcely constructive in nature. The so-called Prescott Commission regretted that their report was "adverse," and their announced, over-all impression was that the university had grown too fast without continuous expert planning over a long period before the admission of students and that its "present method

113

of organization and administration is not consistent with that of a modern educational institution of the university type." A second commission that same year was no less negative in its findings, contending in addition that the "staff lacked evidence of academic calibre, . . . the curriculum showed lack of systematic planning, and the system of examinations was unduly complicated."[28]

The university's increasing need for financial assistance from the government, together with the desire by the state authorities to prevent possible subversion of the institution by communistic or Chinese communal forces, led to further exchange of views between the two parties during the early 1960s. Finally in June 1964 an arrangement was entered into "by which the preservation of Nanyang's identity was assured and the Government would give financial support to the University on the same basis as in the case of the University of Singapore, the state university."[29] The presence on the campus in an important administrative post of an understanding former member of the government's Ministry of Education seemed a relatively small price to pay for an effective working relationship between the government and the university.

The creation by the university of a Curriculum Review Committee in January 1965 was clearly an effort to further such cooperation and at the same time was an attempt by the university administration to improve its service to both students and the community. This committee, subsequently known as the Wang Gungwu Committee after its chairman, a professor of history at the University of Malaya, consisted of faculty members from a number of institutions of collegiate rank as well as representatives of the government, and after four months of extensive research and deliberation, they brought in a report which was to have far-reaching consequences on the future of Nanyang. Although the stated purpose of the committee was to review "the current organisation of courses of study and contents of individual courses . . . and to recommend revised courses of study adapted to the needs of our society,"[30] its more important recommendations were focused on matters of general university organization.

Foremost in its effect on the students was a proposal to shift from the four-year undergraduate program then in existence to a three-year pass-degree structure, to be followed by a one-year honors degree course for pass-degree graduates of outstanding scholastic merit. This change, together with the accompanying plan of establishing tutorials in undergraduate courses, had the effect of providing greater conformity between Nanyang's degree structure and that of the United Kingdom and of the other universities in Singapore and Malaysia, but it also became a basis of contention between students and the administration after its adoption.

A series of recommendations in the Wang Gungwu Report, with respect to language instruction in Nanyang, proceed from basic assumptions as to the multiracial character of Malaysian society.

> . . . there is an urgent need for people with a deep, rational and sympathetic understanding of the multi-racial basis of the country. The University should produce graduates able to guide the course of the country's development, and trained to administer the public services and manage the growth of commerce and industry, and specially equipped to meet the nation's need for rapid modernisation.
>
> We therefore believe that particular attention must be paid to the problem of necessary language skills. It should be the aim of the University to produce graduates who are at least bi-lingual, if not tri-lingual, in the languages relevant to the development of the country.[31]

A major criticism of the committee was that the university had up to that point catered only to students from the Chinese-medium middle schools in Malaysia and that the existing policy of producing graduates proficient only in Chinese was not in the interests of either the students themselves or the country. In this connection, it was recommended that a special Language Center be created

116

for teaching all elementary and intermediate language courses in the university and that "the National Language be given full recognition by the immediate establishment of a Department of Malay Studies."

Still another area of central concern in the evaluation of any university--undoubtedly one of the most critical, namely, the faculty--was given considerable attention by the Wang Gungwu Committee, but this was also the aspect of Nanyang's experience most difficult to alter significantly. The committee specified the securing of "strong Professional Heads" for all twelve departments of the three colleges and the Language Center as the "one key feature" of their recommendations. A separate chapter on teaching staff included as its first and basic proposition: "We feel strongly that courses should be taught by members of the staff with the necessary research experience, preferably with publications . . . in learned journals or original studies published as books or monographs." The usual criteria of British and American institutions of higher learning--academic degrees, years of teaching experience, and research publications-- were indicated as the appropriate bases for granting status in the academic hierarchy, but there was also recognition that salary structures would have to be revised to make them comparable with those in other universities in the region if these standards were to have any real significance. The implication in the report that the teaching staff should be recruited increasingly from among its own graduates is justified ostensibly on the grounds of sheer necessity and of the deeper understanding they would have of conditions in the region, but such a policy would also run counter to the central emphasis in the report on multiracialism. The necessity of providing library facilities adequate to the teaching and research requirements of the institution was also recognized, but in this, as in other of their recommendations, the achievement of the goal was dependent upon many other contingencies, like funds and imaginative and energetic personnel.

With the stimulus of the carefully conceived recommendations of the Wang Gungwu Committee as a guide and the prospect of full recognition by the government of Nanyang graduates, conscientious efforts were made by the administration to upgrade the quality of the university, with varying degrees of success and consequences. Among the numerous recommendations of the Curriculum Review Committee which have been at least partially effectuated are the establishment of the Language Center with instruction in a variety of modern languages, in-

118

cluding English, Malay, and Chinese, the shift to
the three-year pass-degree and fourth-year honors
program, the initiation of tutorials in conjunction
with undergraduate courses, and the establishment
of a Department of Malay Studies--all of which have
influenced student attitudes to a considerable
degree (cf. chapter 5). The establishment during
1970 of a program of graduate studies promises to
have significant consequences in the future.

No adequate criteria exist by which to judge
the tone and quality of an institution such as
Nanyang University, much less to measure the changes
which occur in these respects over a relatively
brief period of time. In any case, this is not the
purpose of the present study, although chapter 5
will provide some indication of students' reactions
to certain aspects of their institutional environment. As a parenthetical note to the present discussion, however, it may be useful to offer one
limited indication of the state of the university
in one of its most critical areas, namely, the
academic quality of its faculty. Although the attainment of advanced degrees is certainly no infal-
lible guide to a person's capabilities in teaching
or research, it is one objective criterion almost
universally applied for acceptance at any but the
lowest positions on a university faculty.

The calendar listing of the entire number of 121 persons on the teaching staff in 1969-1970 indicates that 44 had acquired a doctorate, 58 a master's degree, with 18 having a bachelor's degree or its equivalent. The proportion of those with advanced degrees was naturally higher among faculty at the level of professor or associate professor, with 60.2 percent having received the doctorate, 32.8 percent, the master's degree, and the remaining 7.2 percent, the bachelor's degree. In the Faculty of Science, all but 3 of the 22 persons at the level of professor or associate professor had earned their doctorates. Contrary to a widely held assumption, only 11 of the 102 faculty members with advanced degrees had attained them in Chinese universities, either in precommunist or Nationalist China or Hongkong, while the great majority were obtained either in Europe or America. Although the university has not yet attained the standard of academic training among its faculty that was set by the 1965 report, the level already reached is highly creditable.

Undoubtedly the one most important single development, by way of giving Nanyang University a firm and internationally reputable footing among institutions of higher learning, was the recruiting and installation in 1969 of a widely known and

120

recognized scholar as the Vice Chancellor. On the
basis of developments at Nanyang since its founding,
but especially those since 1965 and its prospects
for the future, the Singapore government, through
its Minister of Education, announced in May 1968
its formal recognition of degrees conferred by the
university. Such official gestures, of course,
cannot erase the memory of earlier stormy encounters
on the Nanyang campus or the doubts as to the competence of Nanyang graduates which long-standing
rumors have implanted, but for the first time in its
history of less than two decades, this university
has in the 1970s the capable leadership and sufficiently favorable working conditions to afford a
reasonable assurance of success.

Products of a Chinese University

The circumstances and the social setting in which
Nanyang University was founded and developed had
been such, until the middle 1960s, as to lead most
outside observers to conclude that the graduates
must be completely Chinese in language and culture,
largely with communist sympathies, and possessing
only mediocre competence in any field of specialization. About as generous an evaluation as any
states that:

> Nanyang had a rather unhappy history in
> its early years by reason of uncertain
> academic standards, mediocre staff and

an inward-looking concentration on all things Chinese. It thus perpetuated at a higher level the drawbacks of the Chinese secondary schools from which it drew its students.[32]

One American political scientist, whose experience as a visiting member of the Nanyang faculty in 1963-1964 had apparently not been a particularly happy one, claimed that the social atmosphere in the university was "stridently chauvinistic," giving "many observers the impression that the university was and from its inception had been but a pawn in Peking's scheme to manipulate the Overseas Chinese for its own ends."

> Many of the grievances, fears and aspirations of Malayan and Singapore Chinese as a whole seem from the beginning to have been reflected in accentuated form by Nanyang's volatile student body. For example, in his contact with numerous students the present writer again and again has been impressed by their quiet but unshaken assumption of Chinese cultural superiority, especially in relation to the Malays, along with resentment that Chinese culture as well as their own advancement is being threatened by various government educational policies that allegedly seek to minimize the Chinese language emphasis in private Chinese schools, and by discrimination in public service appointments.[33]

Another American political scientist was scarcely any more favorably impressed.

> The university has also had constant trouble with excessive control by its financial backers and by student agitators, threatening academic freedom. Student demonstrations have

forced the government to send riot
squads into the campus several times.
Difficulty in getting first-rate staff
has contributed to low standards and
ultimately to problems in placing students. The situation was partly improved when the Singapore government
recognized Nanyang degrees and gave
scholarships. The university continues
as a bulwark of Chinese nationalism
against integration into Malaysian society.[34]

Writing in 1962, an Australian journalist,

with considerable experience in Malaysia, was even

more devastating in his appraisal of Nanyang and

its students, and his predictions for the future

for Singapore and Malaysia were decidedly grim, if

the university were permitted to continue turning

out graduates, of such caliber as he conceived

them to be at that time.[35] While paying tribute

to the physically attractive campus and buildings

in their spacious rural setting, he was chiefly

impressed, as most of the other foreign observers

had been, by the supposedly low academic quality

of the university's instruction and consequently

of its degrees, and the Chinese chauvinism and

communism engendered among the students. He con-

cluded, therefore, that Nanyang had no rightful

place in a multiracial society--that it constituted

instead a danger spot for the nation and the re-

gion. The point of view of the perceptive Chinese-

European writer, Han Suyin, who lectured at Nanyang

in the early 1960s, was also cited to reenforce his contention that the students were so emotionally pro-Chinese that only government control of the university would save it from becoming even more of an instrument of Chinese communism.

There are unfortunately no means of testing the validity of such critical evaluations, which are after all the subjective judgments of outside observers, no matter how objective or well-informed they are supposed to be. The evidence actually presented in most of the accounts indicate a minimum of first-hand investigation and a reliance on impressions current in the community. The ultimate test, of course, is the performance of the students and graduates of the university. Additional light on the outlook of the present students will be provided in succeeding chapters. Although the amount of information relating to Nanyang graduates is less than might be desired, at least a partial answer to basic questions is provided in a study conducted in October 1969 by the Department of Student Affairs among the 4,292 graduates of the university during the decade just ended.[36] In a 20 percent sample of alumni who responded to a mailed questionnaire, 72.6 percent reported that they were employed, either fulltime or parttime, while another 11.4 percent were pursuing further studies,

124

6 percent were involved in military service, and 9.8 percent listed themselves as unemployed--17.8 percent of the women graduates and 7.5 percent of the men.[37]

Considering the brief period of Nanyang University's existence and the stormy nature of its early years, the graduates have already become established in a remarkably wide and significant range of occupations and community functions. Even within this limited sample of its graduates, there are well over a hundred different occupational categories represented, although the great majority may be classified within the five major fields of education (49.6 percent), industry (12.4 percent), government service (11.4 percent), commerce (10.7 percent), and money and banking (9.0 percent). Included in the long list of economic activities in which the graduates engaged were such diverse titles as auditor, credit officer, research executive, high-school teacher, news editor, draftsman, clerk, engineer, factory superintendent, film censor, government economist, interpreter, broker, military officer, and chemist, to mention only a few. The financial returns from these positions were correspondingly varied, ranging from a low of S$200 per month for a clerk or secretary to S$1,700 per month for a research associate and unquestionably much higher in the case of graduates engaged in a personal or family enterprise.

The high proportion of the graduates employed in some form of educational activity involved 44.7 percent of all the men in the sample and 71.8 percent of the women, the latter being engaged chiefly in teaching at the high-school level, while the men ranged from high-school teachers to college lecturers, professors, and administrators.[38] It is quite probable that the traditional Chinese emphasis upon scholarship and the resulting concentration of Nanyang students in the Arts College, especially during the early period of the university's development, contributed substantially to the high proportion of graduates finding occupational outlets in the field of education. So also Nanyang alumni, by virtue of their special competence in Chinese and many of them having graduated from secondary schools in the Chinese stream, enjoyed a special advantage for the posts as teachers in such schools in Singapore. On the other hand, as many of the undergraduate students contend, it is possible that teaching is a last resort for those graduates who, because of linguistic or other deficiencies, lose out in the competition for preferred positions in other fields.

A significantly high proportion of the graduates in this sample (38.2 percent) had pursued further studies in the hopes of qualifying thereby for better occupational opportunities. The largest number had gone to Canada for advanced training, with the second largest number in Singapore, followed by the United States, the United Kingdom, New Zealand, and Taiwan, in that order. A very much smaller proportion of the sample (6.3 percent) had qualified for higher degrees--32 for a master's and 21 for a doctorate--although an additional 67 persons were, at the time of the survey, still engaged in working toward such degrees. Evidence of a serious "brain-drain," although possibly no greater than among the graduates of Singapore University, is indicated by the fact that nearly a third of those who had gone abroad for advanced training had chosen to remain abroad, chiefly because of more and better opportunities. However, the overwhelming majority of the employed Nanyang graduates (93 percent) had remained and invested their competence in the region from which they derived their earlier training, that is, predominantly in Singapore and to a lesser degree in Malaysia. The establishment in 1970 of a new College of Graduate Studies at Nanyang University with four constituent institutes for Asian Studies, Mathematics, Natural Sciences, and Business Studies

127

will enable a larger number of students to obtain additional technical training at home rather than face the costs and complications of going abroad.

There are unfortunately no wholly satisfactory means of ascertaining how well the graduates of Nanyang have been able to adjust to life in their respective communities. On the basis of the survey of graduates just cited, it would appear that nearly one out of every ten of the respondents were unemployed, whether by choice or from lack of acceptable openings. Difficulty in obtaining employment was most commonly attributed especially to the low evaluation placed on Nanyang degrees in the past, and the lack of practical work experience or facility in English on the part of the graduates. While recognizing the limitations of a heavily academic university training as the principal qualification in applying for employment, the great majority (86 percent) of the respondents testified to the value of their education at Nanyang as providing up-to-date knowledge, and in enabling them to discover and develop their own potentials. The listing of the Nanyang graduates on the teaching, administrative, or research staffs, not only of their own alma mater, but also of Singapore University, Singapore Teachers' Training College, and of institutions of higher learning in Malaysia, Hongkong, Mexico,

128

Australia, Canada, and the United States is a reflection of the substantial undergraduate preparation they had obtained. Some indication of the role of Nanyang alumni in the economic and political life of Singapore can also be derived from the reference in the directory to occupations such as "executive" in various departments and bureaus of the Singapore government, "Chief Editor of the Peoples' Action Party," "Executive Engineer" of a public utility, "Head of Propaganda and Publication" of daily newspapers, and "manager" or "superintendent" of banks and numerous economic enterprises.

Notes

1. The two Chinese terms Nan Yang may be literally translated as south or southern and ocean or seas, and the single term Nanyang has long been understood to refer to the region to the south of China, commonly known as Southeast Asia.

2. Guy Hunter, South-East Asia--Race, Culture, and Nation (London, 1966), p. 41.

3. Victor Purcell, The Chinese in Malaya (London, 1967), p. 73.

4. Hsieh Yu-Wei, "The Status of the Individual in Chinese Ethics," in Charles A. Moore (editor), The Chinese Mind: Essentials of Chinese Philosophy and Culture (Honolulu, 1967), p. 310.

5. Lin Yutang, My Country and My People (New York, 1935), p. 222.

6. Dr. Lim Boon Keng in the Straits Chinese Magazine, as quoted in Donald and Joanna Moore, op. cit., p. 474.

7. It was estimated in 1954 that only one out of

every six Chinese primary-school graduates entered the higher grades. Norton Ginsburg and
Chester F. Roberts, Jr., _Malaya_ (Seattle,
1958), p. 307.

8. Gwee Yee Hean, "Education and the Multi-Racial
Society," in Ooi Jin-Bee and Chiang Hai Ding
(editors), _Modern Singapore_ (Singapore, 1969),
p. 209.

9. _Ibid._

10. Donald and Joanna Moore, _One Hundred Fifty
Years of Singapore's History_ (Singapore, 1969),
pp. 493-494.

11. Purcell, _op. cit._, p. 209.

12. _Nanyang University Calendar,_ 1969-1970 (Singapore, 1969), p. 11.

13. _Ibid._

14. It was even suggested by some of its promoters
that the creation of a Chinese University in
Singapore might serve the useful purpose of
discouraging the further exodus of Nanyang
youth back to China for their advanced education. Cf. Richard Butwell, "A Chinese University for Malaya," _Pacific Affairs,_ XXVI, No. 4
(December, 1953), 344-345.

15. Justus M. van der Kroef, _Communism in Malaysia
and Singapore_ (The Hague, 1967), p. 57.

16. Robert S. Elegant, _The Dragon's Seed: Peking
and the Overseas Chinese_ (New York, 1967),
pp. 35, 78.

17. Alex Josey, _Lee Kuan Yew_ (Singapore, 1968),
pp. 421-422.

18. Government White Paper, _Communism in the Nanyang University_ (Kuala Lumpur, 1964), p. 3.

19. Butwell, _op. cit._, p. 345.

20. Government White Paper, _op. cit._, pp. 1-2.

21. Kroef, _op. cit._, p. 38.

22. Government White Paper, _op. cit._, p. 5.

23. James W. Gould, The United States and Malaysia (Cambridge, Massachusetts, 1969), p. 191.

24. Lee Kuan Yew, quoted in Alex Josey, op. cit., pp. 125-126.

25. Ibid., p. 143.

26. According to a visiting American professor of political science at Nanyang, who was decidedly critical of the university, "only about a third or so of Nanyang's student body was /1963-1964/ and is /1967/ politically active," and obviously only a very much smaller group constituted the organizing core, but he insisted that they had succeeded by 1961 in bringing the Nanyang University Student Union, to which every student automatically belonged, "in close alliance with the Barisan Sosialis."--Justus M. van der Kroef, op. cit., p. 58.

27. Government White Paper, op. cit., p. 21.

28. Ibid., p. 4.

29. Nanyang University Calendar, 1969-1970, p. 14.

30. Wang Gungwu and others, Report of the Nanyang University Curriculum Review Committee (Singapore, 1965), p. 1.

31. Ibid., p. 1.

32. J. M. Gullick, Malaysia (New York, 1969), p. 267.

33. Kroef, op. cit., pp. 57-58.

34. James W. Gould, The United States and Malaysia (New York, 1969), p. 191.

35. Ronald McKie, The Emergence of Malaysia (New York, 1963), pp. 275-276, 287.

36. Ong Teck Heng, A Survey of the Occupational Status of Nanyang University Graduates (Singapore, 1970).

37. There is no evidence in the report as to how representative the 836 persons who responded to the questionnaire were of the entire group of 4,292 to whom it was sent, but despite this limitation, the returns do cast some

131

greatly needed light.

38.   Notable in this connection is the fact that al-
      though 40.5 percent of all the employed gradu-
      ates in the sample resided in Malaysia, only
      27.1 percent of those engaged in teaching lived
      in Malaysia, all of whom were teachers at the
      high-school level. This, of course, gives
      further substance to the impression among the
      students, mentioned earlier, of their en-
      countering extra difficulties in seeking
      occupational outlets in Malaysia because of
      their Chinese ancestry and their association
      with a Chinese university.

4

PERSONAL RESOURCES FOR A MULTIRACIAL SOCIETY

Probably the most widely accepted justification for
supporting institutions of higher learning in the
modern world is derived from the assumption that
persons who come under the influence of a university will more than compensate society for its out-
lay on their behalf by the special contributions
they make to the community's welfare. This is perhaps even more evident in developing societies than
technologically advanced ones, since the former
must necessarily scrutinize more closely their
expenditures in terms of the benefits they yield.
Certainly this has been the case in Singapore in
the period since Independence where clear-sighted
administration, faced with extremely limited
sources of income, has recognized the necessity of
testing most carefully the pragmatic value of its
outlays.

Special care with respect to government support
for institutions of higher learning is required in
the case of such multiracial societies as Singapore
because of the university's critical potential as
either a diversive or a unifying agency in the community. If such an educational institution were

to reflect only the interests of one segment of the plural society, no matter how large that portion of the population might be or the amount of support received from that source, the effect obviously could be disastrous to any government that claimed to be built on popular and democratic support.

The problem of how to cultivate personnel with maximum capabilities to serve the interests of the entire community is of course closely associated with the question of how the general population conceive of themselves. Do they think of themselves as belonging primarily to the land to which they or their ancestors had migrated or are their deepest loyalties still to the life and the land from which their ancestors had at one time sprung? This uncertainty may become peculiarly acute and a sensitive issue where, as in Singapore, a predominantly Chinese population is completely surrounded by peoples and nations with traditions and values so markedly different. The basic conception of the state or nation assumes that those who accept its protection and other benefits will also acknowledge their obligation to honor its laws, but does this necessarily imply a complete renunciation of regard for and loyalty to the virtues of the land of one's ancestral origins?

134

Regardless of the way in which this issue may be defined legally or logically, people the world over do derive special satisfaction from the performance of traditional practices and in showing respect for the ways of men in lands they may have never seen but in which their forefathers lie buried. The simple reasoning basic to such behavior was succinctly stated by a prominent Chinese leader of Singapore:

> It is impossible to cut adrift from a nation all its traditions and yet expect it to prosper; a tree severed from its roots, must wither away and degenerate.[1]

People nurtured in a peasant environment find it easy to believe that life and all that is pleasant within it have been derived from their ancestors and the guardian spirits in the land of their forefathers, and this same faith may be transmitted with some success to their children and grandchildren born in distant lands.

The experience of formerly colonialized nations, such as the United States and Canada, reveals that the complete acceptance of the ideals of the land of one's birth by children of immigrants, once commonly taken for granted, may later be seriously questioned by those who contend that "blood runs deeper than water." The "search for personal identity," which supposedly underlies so much of the

unrest of youth within the impersonalized atmosphere of urban centers around the world in recent
years, has found some positive expression in the
widely noted resurgence of interest among third-
and fourth-generation immigrants in the cultures of
their Old-World ancestors.

Multiracialism at the University Level

Singapore, as one of the infant nations of the
world, has sought to resolve the issue of possible
divided loyalty among its peoples by a compromise
of sorts in the official policy of multiracialism.
Under this arrangement, each of the major immigrant groups--Chinese, Indian, and Malay--and a
minor group in numbers but major in power and
influence--the British--were equally recognized
and permitted, if not definitely encouraged, to
retain their separate identity in mode of life
and language, while rendering service and loyalty
to their adopted nation. It is obvious, however,
that a conflict in allegiance may still persist,
however it is resolved in theory, and the difficulty of finding a satisfactory solution undoubtedly reaches its climax at the level of university education, where the preliminary selection
of personnel for critical posts in the nation takes
place. Hence, the bitter resistance in some quar-
ters to a university which seemed at the outset to

136

have a high proportion of its students under Chinese communist influence.

After Nanyang's reorganization, beginning in 1965 and involving a greater degree of control over the internal affairs of the university by government through its contribution to the budget and its representation at the administrative level, the earlier communist threat appeared to subside, at least in the comments of outside observers. But the possible threat of Chinese communalism or chauvinism, as it was so commonly called, could not be disregarded readily or ignored in a student body almost exclusively Chinese undergoing instruction predominantly in Mandarin, and this continues to be a basis for doubts by some.

The government's espousal of multiracialism as a national ideal, however, would seem to justify the acceptance and support of a university whose principal medium of instruction was in one of four officially recognized languages of the nation, providing it also opened its doors to qualified students regardless of their ancestry. It was not illogical, therefore, that the Prime Minister, who had so frequently emphasized in his public statements the necessity of providing equal treatment before the law for all persons regardless of their racial antecedents, should also stress the desir-

137

ability of preserving some of the peculiar elements derived most markedly from any one of the constituent racial groups. So, for example, in speaking to the students of Nanyang University in October 1966, Lee Kuan Yew could consistently contend that there was something special in Chinese culture which was needed for society's survival, and which, he implied, it was Nanyang's duty to help preserve. While recognizing the dangers, particularly among the Chinese, of becoming disdainful or contemptuous in their relations with people from other racial backgrounds--of assuming that the supreme benefits of their own culture could be appreciated only by those who had been born to the part--the Chinese should expect to retain their ethnic identity.

Early in 1966 Lee had told the students of Nanyang that "in Singapore, Malaya, Sabah, Sarawak, and Indonesia the descendants of the Chinese will be identifiable from the other races even a hundred years from now. They find it very, very difficult to be assimilated completely with the indigenous peoples. This is not because of language and culture, but more because of religion, a very important factor."[2] Later in the same year in addressing the Nanyang students, Lee suggested that the growing disposition of the Chinese in Singapore to send their children "to English schools for

138

plain bread-and-butter reasons" might have the unfortunate effect of producing "anaemic, up-rooted
floating citizens without the social cohesiveness
and the cultural impetus that gives peoples the
drive and the will to succeed as a group."[3]

Long before Nanyang University had been
recognized by the government as having a legitimate
role in the education for leadership among the large
proportion of secondary students whose training
had been primarily in the Chinese language, the
University of Malaya (now the University of Singapore) had acquired status as the main and virtually
the only center for higher education in both the
Federation and Singapore. Founded in 1949 through
a merging of the Raffles College of Arts and the
King Edward VII College of Medicine, the university
enjoyed the distinction from the outset of government recognition and financial support and instruction in the English language. Thus, only students
with competence in the English language and in
other academic skills derived chiefly from schools
in the English stream were able to secure admission,
but the great majority of the students nevertheless
had been of Chinese ancestry. The prestige acquired
by the University of Singapore from its earlier
founding, its initial higher standards of admission
and instruction, and its greater financial support

139

and wider selection of faculty, continues to be taken for granted among many observers, although the distinctions in the competence of the graduates of the two institutions--the University of Singapore and Nanyang University--are known to be much less now than they were a decade ago and they are becoming still less with the passage of time. The greater facility among the students of the University of Singapore over those at Nanyang to communicate in the English language obviously gives the former an advantage in contact with the outside world.[4]

The issue of the language to be used as the medium of instruction and communication for the prospective leadership of the country has certainly not been wholly resolved, and this necessarily reflects itself in the relative attraction of the two universities in Singapore. The present-day political leaders of the country, who during the struggle for independence advocated so strongly for the use of Asian languages rather than English, have, of course, recognized the preeminence of the latter as the broader medium of trade, as well as of literature. Lee Kuan Yew, who, like most of the other dominant political figures in Singapore of the 1960s, had received his basic education in English schools and his university training in

140

England, was impelled in 1956 under the dominant anticolonial spirit of the day to state that his son was not going to an English school to become a "model Englishman." He further stated that Chinese and Malay were destined to be the dominant languages of Malaya, and yet it could be argued that:

> Singapore survived as a democracy because the English-educated, led by Lee Kuan Yew, defeated the more left-wing Chinese-educated to produce an energetic, progressive government which was ready to work, as the government of an independent sovereign state, with Western technology, and with European nations, as well, as with noncommunist Asia, while maintaining a neutralist attitude toward states of all ideologies.[5]

Certainly the leadership in the administration of Singapore as an independent nation and in positions of major responsibility for the phenomenal economic expansion of the country during the modern period are quite competent in the English language in addition to any ancestral language they may possess. Moreover the increasing tendency among Chinese parents to send their children to primary schools using both English and Chinese,[6] means that in the not distant future, the selection by qualified students of either Nanyang University or the University of Singapore would no longer be determined by the fact that the former uses Chinese as the major medium of instruction while the latter uses English.

The fact that Nanyang University continues to use Chinese as its principal medium of communication and that for some years its students will not have comparable facility in the English language will unquestionably color the conceptions and the expectations which the general public develops toward the institution and its students. In an economy, which in Singapore's setting and circumstances is so greatly dependent upon technological and managerial skills, the public is increasingly disposed to judge the university and its students on pragmatic rather than ideological grounds--on how its graduates can perform in the professions, industry, or administration rather than on how they react toward communal or communistic issues. This does not mean, however, that questions of racial solidarity or the many other problems of their relationships to the world about them have little significance to either the students or the public, or that they may not also figure prominently for many Singaporeans in the near future.

A Nanyang Student Profile

The theory commonly held in official circles, at least, that the leadership of any country in the modern world is likely to be drawn preponderantly from among persons with a university education, suggests the desirability of examining somewhat

142

more closely the character of the student body at
Nanyang University. In a community consisting so
overwhelmingly of Chinese, there could be special
significance in anticipating the potential leadership of the future from an analysis of even the most
general information of Nanyang's screening of students, drawn as it so largely is from among graduates of Chinese middle schools. Many of the following data are taken from official records as reported
in the university calendar for various years from
1959 to 1970, although the more detailed information is derived from the 1969 survey.

The original expectation of the founders that
Nanyang would provide an opportunity for higher
education to the Chinese throughout the entire
region of Southeast Asia has, of course, never been
fully realized. It was much more nearly approximated during the earlier years of the institution's
history, in the sense that then the greater proportion of the students came from outside Singapore, whereas in recent years the situation has
been reversed. In 1961, the majority of the students (61 percent) were recruited from areas other
than Singapore--chiefly from Malaya (55.6 percent)
and the remainder from Sabah, Sarawak, Brunei, and
Indonesia, but including a small number from Thailand and Taiwan. Singapore's establishment as a

143

separate nation in 1965 and the consequent granting
of special subsidies to its citizens brought about
a gradual decline in the number of students from
outside the island and an increase of those from
within--the outside proportion dropping to 38.1
percent in 1967 and still further to 14.6 percent
in 1970. A noteworthy difference between the Nanyang students drawn from Singapore as compared with
those recruited outside the island is that the
former to a much greater degree than the latter have
tended to concentrate in the "liberal" disciplines
in the College of Arts, while the students from
other parts of Southeast Asia have more frequently
and consistently specialized in the natural and
physical sciences and the applied fields in the
College of Commerce. One of the significant developments in the closing years of the 1960s was
the beginning of a more truly international tinge
to the student body, with a small representation
in 1970, chiefly for Chinese studies, from Taiwan,
Russia, Japan, the United States, Hongkong, Thailand, Australia, France, Sweden, and Israel. This
small proportion of students from areas outside the
region (34 in the total enrollment of 2,233 in
1970) will almost certainly rise during the 1970s
and should help to broaden the perspective of the
much larger group of students from within South-

144

east Asia.

The high but declining proportion of men among Nanyang's students, averaging between three to four men for every woman in the earlier years but dropping to a two-to-one ratio in 1969-1970, obviously reflects the shifting status of the two sexes with respect to higher education within the Chinese communities of Southeast Asia.[7] The traditional expectation among the Chinese that their daughters would sooner or later marry out and that family prestige and status would not be enhanced by sacrificing for their advanced education, probably still prevails to a marked degree even among the urbanized peoples of Singapore, although it also seems to be declining slowly. Throughout the entire period, the disproportion between the sexes has been, as one would expect, significantly lower among the students from Singapore than among those from elsewhere in Malaysia or other parts of Southeast Asia, parents from outside the city being hesitant to send their daughters so far from home.

The expected tendency of women to specialize in the arts and humanities was even more noticeable among the severely restricted student body in 1961 than among the expanded number in 1969--60 percent of the 435 women in the university being so enrolled in 1961 as against 44.5 percent of the 677 women

145

at the end of the decade. Less than half of the
men (46.2 percent) were registered in the College
of Arts in 1961 and this ratio had dropped to 29.9
percent by the end of the decade.[8] On the other
hand, in certain fields, such as Chinese studies and
history, the women were by 1969 almost as well represented as the men, although in the sciences their
small numbers in proportion to the men were still
very marked--approximating a ratio of 1 female to
every 9 males in physics, and 1 to 3 in chemistry
and mathematics. In the honors program, which had
just been initiated, the ratio of men to women was
roughly 6 to 1, and would certainly not be regarded
as an accurate reflection of the relative capability
of the two sexes for advanced training (see Table
6).

For information regarding the other numerous
attributes of the Nanyang student body which shed
light on their present orientation to life and on
what may be expected of them in the future, the
1969 survey provides our best single source. The
survey reveals, as one would expect, that the great
bulk of the students (89.7 percent) fall in the
five-year age span from 18 to 22 inclusive and that
the median age is 20.6 years. In this respect
there is nothing exceptional in the experience of
the Nanyang students, and even the range among the

146

Table 6
Composition of the Nanyang Student Body, 1961-1968

College	1 9 6 1			1 9 6 8		
	Male	Female	Total	Male	Female	Total
Arts	703	261	964	393	301	694
	(35.9)	(13.3)	(49.2)	(19.4)	(14.9)	(34.3)
Science	571	119	690	532	191	723
	(29.1)	(6.1)	(35.2)	(26.3)	(9.4)	(35.7)
Commerce	251	55	306	426	181	607
	(12.7)	(2.8)	(15.5)	(21.1)	(8.9)	(30.0)
Total	1,525	435	1,960	1,351	673	2,024*
	(77.7)	(22.2)	(99.9)	(66.7)	(33.3)	(100.0)

Note: Numerals in parentheses indicate percentages.
*Excludes Language Center.

remaining 10.3 percent from a low of 15 years to a
high of 44 years is not unusual, considering the
fact that most of those over age 28 were non-
Chinese.

The average size of the Nanyang student's
family is very large, as judged by Western standards, and it is high even as compared with the entire Chinese population of Singapore in 1966. According to data from the Singapore Sample Household
Survey, 1966, the median size of Chinese households
of single nuclear families was 4.83 persons, whereas among the families of the students, the median
number of siblings alone--not including the par-
ents--was 5.75 persons. Although these figures are

147

not strictly comparable in several respects, their juxtaposition serves to emphasize the simple fact that the average families of Nanyang students are large and to suggest that the attitudes and conduct of the students may be influenced thereby. One-seventh of the students come from families which by any standard must be regarded as large--ten or more children. Further the fact that the Nanyang students in 1969 tended to be among the older siblings in their families, with 22.0 percent of them being the eldest child and another 35.3 percent being either the second or third oldest child, may have served to place upon them an added sense of family obligation. Certainly the impression likely to be derived, from even limited association on the campus, is that of a student body which has been largely nurtured in a Chinese environment, either of Singapore or some other part of Malaysia.[9]

For example, the overwhelming majority of students in the survey (96.8 percent) had their primary education in Chinese schools, and only a somewhat smaller preponderance of the students (91.7 percent) had their secondary education in Chinese schools. The small group of less than 1 percent whose initial instruction was in Malay schools were of Malayan ancestry and enrolled in the Department of Malay Studies. The remaining small

148

minority had been trained in schools, either at the primary or secondary level, in which English, Malay, or a combination of these with Chinese had been the medium of instruction.

The direct impact of China on the Nanyang students is perhaps best reflected in the high proportion of their family members actually born in China. One out of every eight students (12.4 percent) were themselves natives of China, and, considering their age, most of them were born there during or after the communist revolution. Equally or even more significant is the fact that the fathers of six out of every eight (77.2 percent) students in the survey and the mothers of five out of every eight (62.4 percent) were born in China, suggesting how direct and intimate this old-country influence would be on the great majority of the students.[10] It could be assumed that the Chinese atmosphere of the neighborhoods in Singapore, Malaysia, or Indonesia in which the great majority of the students were born or which they still regard as their home, may have been equally compulsive or restrictive as in the villages of South China from which their parents or some of their classmates may have come.

The existence, on the other hand, of a significant portion of Nanyang's students whose grandpar-

ents had been born outside of China reflects the
possibility of at least three generations of influences emanating from outside the ancestral land.
It should be noted in this connection that the
students were apparently less well informed regarding the place of birth and residence of their grandparents than might have been expected, coming from
a cultural tradition in which filial piety has
played such a central role. The proportion of students who either neglected to provide these data or
indicated that they did not know was higher on
these questions than on any others in the survey
requiring purely objective answers. Among the
students who were able to report the birthplace of
their grandparents, there were over one-eighth
(13.6 percent) whose maternal grandparents on either
one or both sides had been born outside of China,
while on the paternal side this ratio was somewhat
lower (7.6 percent), owing partly to the higher
ratio of males among the earlier immigrants and the
consequent necessity of finding a wife among the
residents of Singapore or of their postponing
marriage. Slightly over half of the students who
were informed on the subject reported that one or
both of the maternal grandparents were either
living or had died in some part of Southeast Asia,
and somewhat less than half (43.7 percent) of the
150

students gave the same report on their paternal grandparents. Thus, a dual set of cultural controls--one emanating from the ancestral homeland which had been left behind and the other from the mixed cultural setting into which they had migrated--must have operated significantly, although to a varying degree, upon both the families from which the Nanyang students have come and upon the students themselves.

The persistence of ancestral ties and loyalties is further reflected in the identification of the students and their parents with dialectal and provincial groupings from China. Virtually all the students knew and reported to which of eleven designated groups their parents belonged, the great majority of the Chinese indicating one or another of the five most widely represented dialectal groups--Hokkien, Teochew, Hainanese, Cantonese, and Hakka, roughly in that order of magnitude (see Table 7). Although there are no means of knowing how these figures compare with the ratios in the total parental population from which Nanyang students are drawn, there is, as noted in Table 7, a rather striking correspondence in the main with the total Chinese population of Singapore in 1957. The most notable exceptions occur among the Hainanese, who are somewhat overrepresented in the

Table 7
Distribution of Dialectal Groups
of Parents of Nanyang Students

Dialectal Group	Percentage		
	Fathers (1969)	Mothers (1969)	Singapore Chinese Population (1957)
Hokkien	43.7	39.0	40.6
Teochew	21.0	22.6	22.5
Hainanese	12.3	11.0	7.2
Cantonese	9.7	13.8	18.9
Hakka	7.4	8.3	6.7
Shanghainese	1.5	0.9	1.0
Other	4.5	4.2	3.1

Nanyang student body, and the Cantonese, who are even more markedly underrepresented, especially among the fathers of the Nanyang students.[11] It is quite likely that the Cantonese, having arrived in Southeast Asia at an earlier period than the Hainanese, have been able to a great degree to enter their sons or daughters in either the University of Singapore or in other institutions for advanced education overseas.

Although the usual Western criteria for judging economic level or class may not be wholly valid in a situation such as Singapore's where family ties figure so prominently and may be so widely shared, data obtained from the Nanyang students indicate that they come from a wide range of

152

family-income levels and of occupational backgrounds. Assuming that the students are reasonably
well informed and accurate in their reporting, it
would appear that they were drawn chiefly from
middle-income families, with a median monthly
income of S$601.71. This figure may appear moder-
ately high, especially when compared with the very
much lower median-monthly income of S$194.34 per
head of household, reported for the entire population of Singapore in 1966.[12] On the other hand,
such an income could not provide a very high level
of living for the relatively large families of Nanyang students, averaging seven or more persons.
There were some students who felt very keenly the
humiliation associated with the fact that their
families were receiving government assistance.

Nearly half (45.1 percent) of the Nanyang
families derived incomes ranging from S$400 to S$750
per month, while another 37 percent had incomes
exceeding S$750 per month, and 17.9 percent received
less than S$300 per month. The presence in the
student body of a rather large minority (22.7
percent) who believed their family income to be
S$1,000 per month or more and doubtless many with
incomes several times that amount stands out
sharply in contrast with and creates problems for
the sizeable minority of 6.9 percent from families

153

with incomes of less than S$200 per month.

Data on the occupations providing the principal support for the families of Nanyang students further confirm this impression of a rather broad range of income levels, with its corresponding spread in the expectations among the students. For example, one-sixth (16.7 percent) of the students came from families in which manual labor was the chief source of income, while one-tenth came from professional families of doctors, lawyers, scientists, educators, etc. One-fifth (20.7 percent) of the families obtained their major income from the ownership and operation of small shops, and, of course, this could mean either a meager or a highly remunerative occupation. The largest group of students--slightly more than a quarter-- indicated that the chief source of support for the family came from the "owner or senior official of a firm or government agency."

Relatively few of the principal breadwinners in the families of Nanyang students were engaged as craftsmen or operatives (5.5 percent), in service occupations (6.2 percent), or even as sales and clerical workers (15.2 percent). In all of these areas, as well as laborers, the Nanyang families were underrepresented as compared with the distribution of Chinese workers in general in 1966, while

154

they were significantly overrepresented in professional and administrative pursuits.

Undoubtedly one of the important factors,
quite apart from intellectual qualifications which
enable a considerable number of the Nanyang students, particularly from the lower economic levels,
to attend the university is the presence of more
than one wage earner within the family, reenforced
by the strong tradition of family solidarity within
the Chinese community. Somewhat over half (56.7
percent) of the Nanyang households had the support
of two or more "economically active" persons--
29.1 percent by two, 16.1 percent by three, and
the remaining 11.5 percent by from four to nine
family collaborators.

A further indication of a distinct shift in
the social status of many of the families of Nanyang students is provided in data indicating the
difference in the level of formal education attained
by the parents and their children. It is perhaps
a reflection on the limited degree of communication
within their families that an exceptionally high
proportion of the students' professed ignorance as
to the maximum level of formal education attained
by their parents--9.0 percent with respect to their
fathers and 7.5 percent regarding their mothers.
Of those who claimed to have knowledge on this

155

point, more than half of the students stated that
their fathers had not completed primary education
while a fifth (20.7 percent) contended that their
fathers had received no formal education. The
mothers of the students were reported as having even
fewer educational benefits, with nearly half (47.4
percent) having been denied any formal school experience, while another 22.7 percent had not completed even a primary education. Somewhat more
than one-fifth (22.1 percent) of the fathers, as
contrasted with only one-eighth (12.0 percent)
of the mothers, had completed secondary education,
but only a very small minority--6.1 percent of the
fathers and 2.3 percent of the mothers--had completed university or postgraduate training. The marvel
is that parents with meager economic and formal
educational resources of their own and with such
heavy family responsibilities should be disposed
or find it possible to send even one of their children to college. That they have done so is, of
course, a reflection of both the strong intellectual tradition which persists among the Chinese
in Singapore and of a hope that thereby they might
promote the welfare and status of a family.

A surprisingly high level of educational
attainment among the siblings of the Nanyang students further underscores the growing awareness

among the overseas Chinese of the values of higher education, within their own tradition and as the means to economic and social advancement in the new environment. Nearly three-quarters (71.8 percent) of the students reported that their "best-educated brother" had at least finished secondary school, and another quarter (24.6 percent) had graduated from a university or taken additional postgraduate training. Among the sisters of the students, the record of educational achievement is somewhat less impressive but still surprisingly high, with 64.9 percent having completed secondary school and an additional 12.9 percent having attained a college degree or better.

No single sharply defined model or profile of the Nanyang student emerges from the foregoing data. Rather, on virtually all of the objective traits examined thus far--age, major field of specialization in college, place of birth, occupation and income of parents, educational attainments of parents and siblings, etc.--there is evidence of considerable change over a span of time and of a fairly wide range of difference among the students at any one time, with at best some indication of one or more central tendencies.

Some Qualities of Student Character

The effective use which selected persons make of the resources that are available to them depends upon such a wide range of individual qualities and circumstances that it becomes dangerous to generalize, even if all the desired information could be obtained. In a social and economic world destined to undergo such extensive change as Singapore has during the remainder of the twentieth century, it would be folly to attempt any specific projection of character traits which the future will require, and it would be equally hazardous to seek the means of determining how contemporary students might respond to such demands. There are nevertheless in the responses obtained from the Nanyang students in the 1969 survey some unanticipated clues to what might be expected from them in terms of present-day demands.

There was, for example, much more evidence of disagreement with traditional educational practices and points of view, at least as reflected through the anonymous device of the questionnaire, than might have been expected among Nanyang students, who are supposedly so accustomed to "rote learning and respect for the sage." Thus, student expressions of dissatisfaction with various aspects of university life were considerably more

158

frequent than statements of formal acceptance or appreciation. On 18 of the 22 questions relating to campus affairs included in the 1969 survey, the composite scores from the students reflected some degree of disapproval more frequently than of approval.[13]

The presence of a highly individualistic and competitive atmosphere on the campus obviously weighs heavily on the consciousness of the students, as evidenced in the frequency with which this theme appears spontaneously in their comments on quite unrelated topics, and it probably figures significantly in the high proportion of extremely negative reactions to a variety of different aspects of campus experience. Such impersonalized, cutthroat striving, which is perhaps accepted as normal and natural in the world of trade, doubtless appears inappropriate and distinctly unpleasant in a situation of continued face-to-face relations that is assumed to approximate the intimacy of the family.

Again and again in the student comments about classroom procedures, examinations, departmental morale, and especially on the matter of congeniality and friendliness of the students, which was rated as "unsatisfactory" by more than half of the students (56.6 percent), the underlying basis of

the criticism was the disruptive influence of competition.

> Competition is keen so that everybody
> makes scoring his central interest.--
> Science/3M[14]

> The students are certainly very hard
> working, but they study only for
> marks and they are very selfish.--Arts/2/F

> The barriers between students of both
> sexes is too strong; they behave like an
> enemy toward one another.--Business/1/M

> The competition for survival is so keen
> that the students become jealous and
> hostile to one another. Congeniality
> hardly exists. The students are in-
> hibited because of the fear that they
> may suffer in marks.--Science/2/F

> No friendships exist in the examination
> hall, as is the case of a gambling house
> where no blood relations could prevail.--
> Science/4/M

> Students have become slaves to marks and
> consequently disregard friendships.--
> Arts/2/F

> Everybody tries to outdo the other in
> marks, which has become the criterion
> of friendliness. Acquaintance is sought
> where there is advantage to be gained.--
> Arts/1/M[15]

Some students went so far as to mention "critici-
zing of the fellow students" as the subject of
first importance among the topics they discuss in
casual conversation.

Judging by the frequency and the range in
which the problem of such competitive striving was
introduced in the student comments, it would appear
that the entire student body had become involved,

160

many without being particularly conscious that it affected them. At the same time it is clear that strong friendships exist among the students, as occasional written comments indicate, but the dominant competitive atmosphere sometimes tends to discourage too open expression of these friendships lest it be interpreted as a bid for special favors.

Like the Freudian id, the competitive atmosphere and influence makes its presence known in unsuspected places and contexts. For example, a question on departmental morale was largely interpreted in terms of the individual struggle for grades among the students and the consequent alienation from each other rather than in a positive sense of collective striving and support of one another. Repeatedly students gave evidence of being torn between a sense of pride in the achievements of their fellows that resulted from resourcefulness and industry and a realization of the losses in interpersonal relations as a consequence of their individualistic striving.

> Our fellow students are diligent, but unfortunately because of the desire to excel over other in marks, all are in a rat race.--Arts/3/M

> Most students are extremely hard working, but they are concerned only with what is in their textbooks. Being university students, they ought to widen their horizons.--Commerce/1/F

> Learning is strictly an individual
> matter and consists mainly of dead
> memorizing with a hope to top the
> class. There is no effort to help
> out, but only contempt for those
> with poor results and jealousy for
> those with good results.--Science/2/M

It is probably true that most people in the modern world are caught in a similar dilemma of conflicting concerns--for the friendliness and congeniality of small, face-to-face groups like the family, on the one hand, and for the stimulation and excitement of competing for a living and for status within an industrialized setting, on the other hand. These conflicting dispositions and social situations are, of course, no more likely to be resolved for the students of Nanyang, either now or later, than they are for the population of Singapore as a whole, but it would seem that the university setting tends to place a special premium upon the ability to surpass in such individualistic strivings. It would also seem that, because of their especially close family associations, Nanyang students are particularly sensitive to the alienation from their fellows which the competitive atmosphere of the university induces.

The traditional Chinese concern for scholarly prowess, however that is conceived, undoubtedly plays a significant part in the willingness of Nanyang students to accept the objectionable as-

162

pects of the academic "rat race," including a considerable amount of what many of them have come to
regard as meaningless ritualism. Thus, a rather
high proportion of the Nanyang students gave their
teachers a favorable rating with respect to academic training and ability (39.0 percent) and their
enthusiasm in the classroom (41.5 percent) as
contrasted with those who rated them as unsatisfactory in these respects (21.1 and 26.8 percent,
respectively). On the other hand, the percentage
of students who expressed high appreciation for the
stimulation they were deriving from their classes
(28.2 percent) was very much less than that of
those who expressed dissatisfaction (42.8 percent).

The ambivalent nature of the student dispositions in this area--of accepting somewhat
uncritically the pronouncements from the printed
page or the teacher's mouth, and of demanding the
right to question and test the supposed wisdom of
the authorities--is illustrated more vividly in
their scattered comments rather than in the statistical summaries. A second-year student in Chinese
studies seems to accept as inevitable that "the
lecturers are high above while the students are
far below and in between there is a great barrier,"
while other students observe distinctions among the
faculty, but also claim the right to pass judgment

163

on them.

> Some lecturers make it possible for us
> to get more detailed explanations and
> to discuss problems outside the class
> and has enabled us to gain knowledge not
> available in books. Others take offense
> when students put questions which they
> find difficult to answer. They are not
> humble enough to listen to the student's
> view, but cling blindly to their lecture
> notes. Some even dictate their notes;
> it is very boring indeed.--Arts/2/F

> Some are really good and serious in
> teaching and others are simply talking
> rubbish.--Arts/2/F

A student in commerce bemoans both the mechanical
methods and the lack of imagination on the part of
the faculty and the readiness of her associates
to accept such treatment.

> They don't teach us how to think--to
> analyze and solve problems. The lecturers
> churn out their notes without explana-
> tions and the students try hard to memor-
> ize them.--Commerce/2/F

Most students fortunately have become more dis-
criminating in this regard, recognizing that the
faculty vary greatly in their ability to stimulate
different types of students.

Whatever disposition there might be among the
present-day students at Nanyang to rebel overtly
and to take action against "the establishment" in
their campus world, it has not thus far been
directed to any noticeable extent toward the academic system per se. There is evidence in the survey returns of a considerable amount of dissatis-

164

faction among the students with other aspects of their university experience--examination procedures, library facilities, the three-year pass system, tutorials, laboratories and teaching equipment-- but not to the point of their becoming acute sources of conflict or of violent demonstrations.[16] It seems quite probable that their apparent passivity on matters of purely academic procedure is derived in considerable part from their Chinese heritage of deep respect for both the scholarly profession and the academic institution. Thus, the high proportion of the students (62.9 percent) who ex- pressed some degree of disapproval toward the examination system were apparently voicing their protest toward the manner of administration and not toward the principle of determining the right of students to remain in the university or of securing its stamp of approval as graduates on the basis of their performance in examinations. The validity of the system, as such, did not appear to be questioned.

Personal Goals and Objectives

Although each of the two thousand students in at- tendance at Nanyang in 1969 came from a different set of circumstances and capabilities from every other student, there were nevertheless certain com- mon goals toward which they were striving. In

spite of the certainty that these objectives will
change with time and individuals will vary greatly
in their persistence of purpose, some intimation
of their future role and potential may be obtained
from the way in which the students conceive of their
prospects.

Naturally enough, a central concern of students
was directed toward their vocational outlets following their experience at the university. In
answer to a specific question, "In what occupation
are you hoping to enter following graduation from
Nanyang?" slightly more than half (51.3 percent)
indicated that they were "undecided," while the
next highest proportion (17.0 percent) mentioned
"teaching." An equal proportion (14.1 percent),
almost wholly from the college of commerce, were
looking forward to some phase of business--banking,
accountancy, industrial relations, or management--
and the remaining 14.6 percent were divided among
government service (6.7 percent) and a miscellaneous
variety of vocations, including engineering, social
work, journalism, and scientific research. The
fact that a number of the more common professional
fields, such as medicine, dentistry, law, and
religion, were either entirely omitted or listed
only very infrequently, is at least partially at-
tributable to a sense of inadequacy in the English

166

language, which was regarded as essential for advanced technical training.

The failure of such a large proportion of the students to reach a decision regarding their future occupation is quite comprehensible in the light of the dynamic character of the industrialized world in which most of them expect to reside. This indecision with regard to their vocational plans, which is probably also reflected in a similar degree of uncertainty among those who indicated that they had made some choice, sheds light also on the general state of morale in the student body. It obviously has a bearing on the 54.6 percent of the survey respondents who expressed dissatisfaction with what their classroom experience had to offer to their future vocational plans even though more than half of all the students had not yet been able to arrive at a decision.

The dominant impression likely to be derived from a reading of the statements made by the students themselves regarding their vocational prospects is of a persistent and gnawing sense of pessimism. Nearly half (46.3 percent) of the student comments, taken at their face value, were clearly apprehensive, with such terms as grim, bleak, gloomy, or slim appearing repeatedly, while another 30 percent expressed mixed feelings of un-

167

certainty, and a mere fifth of the statements could be classified as positively hopeful or optimistic. The predominantly negative note among young people, whose high enthusiasm and confidence would be what is normally expected, could be interpreted as an expression of honest realism and of a disposition to face unreservedly the difficulties which unquestionably will be encountered. Certainly the general behavior of the students on the campus and their comments on other aspects of the survey do not support an impression of a pervasive gloom or pessimism among them.

Among the majority of the men, the inevitability of a period of military service after graduation not only adds to the uncertainty regarding their vocational prospects, but it also detracts somewhat from the enthusiasm they can bring to bear on their academic pursuits. One can understand some of the academic apathy which might occur as a result of the dilemma posed by one third-year student, but faced by most of the men on the campus, "How useful is my knowledge of economic theory or of government likely to be when I am called up for national service?" A similar logic underlies the frequently expressed skepticism regarding the value of their university training because "all will have been forgotten after

168

three years of national service, which is equivalent to unemployment." This same refrain was repeated in a variety of different ways, especially by science and commerce students who felt that the lapse in time between their graduation from the university and the initiation into their vocation would be too great and that the money and time invested at the university would have been wasted.

A second set of factors contributing to the pessimistic outlook toward their future centered around the language issue and the way this has been defined by the government. The impression appears widespread that Nanyang graduates are invariably rated inferior to the graduates from Singapore University in the competition for jobs with both the government and many business firms, and that this discrimination is chiefly a consequence of a deficient command of the English language and of the associated but questionable notion that the qualification in other respects must likewise be inferior. The varied interpretation of the facts and the temperamental reactions, ranging from deep resentment to fatalistic acceptance, are best reflected in their own words.

> I am quite pessimistic about this. Our
> government has not been able to treat
> graduates of Nanyang and Singapore Uni-
> versity with equality. Our Government
> is too autocratic. They are only dirty,

political game-players and we suffer the
consequences. We, as a matter of fact,
are living in an unequal society. Perhaps our university has its own defects;
its level of English is too low and we
must try our best to improve it.--
Arts/2/M

Since its establishment, Nanyang has
produced numerous graduates, well-trained
and proven to be of equal capabilities to
those of other institutions of higher
learning in Singapore; yet they have been
discriminated against. Is it due to the
fact that they speak Chinese and not English, or that the Chinese graduates do not
measure up to the standards of English-
educated graduates? It is hoped that the
authorities would treat all alike and certainly we don't mean to ask for a bigger
share of favours.--Arts/2/M

The government is partial to an English-
educated staff. That is one of the
reasons that certain staff members are so
rude and bureaucratic. The government
should employ more Chinese-educated staff
in government departments and let them show
their abilities and sincerity. The colonial type of government servants should
not exist.--Science/2/M

We are no match for the Singapore University graduates, not because of our poor
academic performance, but the poor command
of English. We stand to lose out in the
interviews conducted in English.--
Business/1/M

After graduation the employment prospects
are very slim, for there would be graduates with equivalent qualifications from
the University of Singapore and they would
stand a better chance.--Science/2/M

The Nanyang students from Malaysia recognize

even greater handicaps on the basis of their

citizenship, owing to the governmental policy of

giving preference to Malays and of refusing to

recognize the Nanyang degree.

> Because the Malaysian government is racially disposed in her anti-Chinese policy, it looks after the interests of the Malays and does not recognize the Nantah degree. The future prospects are very dim.--Commerce/3/M

> Each Malaysian student at Nanyang suffers the same hard fate. The degree is not recognized by the Malaysian government and the Singapore government is not liberal in granting of permits for them to stay or to work. They are an unwanted group in both countries.--Arts/2/M

A strong note of fatalism, sometimes termed "the besetting sin" of the Chinese, and certainly widely noted in Chinese philosophy,[17] is clearly evident in much of the pessimism expressed by the Nanyang students. The sentiment frequently expressed is that the forces obstructing their future welfare are not only completely beyond personal power to influence or control, as in the excess of supply over demand on the labor market or the settled policy of government, but it is as if the gods themselves had ordained it.

> Life for me is meaningless, for there is no prospect at all that I could fit in at all with either the high-brow or the low-brow jobs.--Arts/2/F

> I believe in fate and who can tell what will happen tomorrow?--Commerce/3/F

> Future prospects can never be predicted, as all depends on fate.--Science/1/M

The fatalistic quality of their pessimism sometimes expresses itself in a less deterministic but equally impersonal fashion as "luck" or "chance." The students, especially the girls, would write of what would happen if their "fortune is good" or if "ill fortune" occurs, much as if it were the outcome of a throw of the dice, but with the usual implication that the odds were against them. An occasional comment, such as "I dare not be optimistic" or "I had best not think about it," suggests a fear that undue optimism might appear presumptuous and tempt the gods to take revenge.

The vigorous denial of luck or fate as determining factors in one's vocational prospects, by a resolute minority of the Nanyang students, is at the same time an evidence of how widespread the sense of pessimistic fatalism is among their fellows, and perhaps unconsciously among themselves. There can be little doubt, however, of the genuine quality of the assurance expressed in the following comments:

> I feel very confident about the future, having obtained the modern language from the University and a mastery of a second and third languages.--Science/2/M

> If I have the ability, and versatility, I need not worry, for although the chances depend very much on luck, still the probability of employment correlates with the amount of talent one has. I disagree with the view that graduation means unemployment. Those who hold such views are either poor in results or are

incapable.--Science/2/M

> It depends on us to improve the environ-
> ment so that we as graduates of a Chi-
> nese university can make even a bigger
> contribution to society and thus dispel
> the discrimination which now exists in
> salaries.--Arts/3/M

> I believe if only I am willing to work
> hard, employment prospects would not be
> a problem. Whether one succeeds or not,
> as I see it, has no direct relation to
> the fact that one is a Nantah graduate.
> It depends on the individual. It is
> likely that two graduates of the same
> department may meet with far different
> opportunities and fare differently
> in life.--Arts/1/M

The confidence for the future among a number of the
students in commerce was derived from their family
connections, with a ready-made position awaiting
them, although understandably this also reenforced
the charge of nepotism among those not possessing
such fortunate kinship ties. There was, in any
case, a feeling that commerce was one field in
which persons of Chinese ancestry and linguistic
competence might enjoy some special advantage.

Additional university training had come to be
recognized by a substantial minority of the students as a possible escape from the handicaps they
foresaw. Nearly a quarter (24.5 percent) of the
students in the survey indicated that they expected "to secure additional university training
after graduation from Nanyang," many of them stating that it would only be with such assistance that

173

they could hope to break into their chosen occupation. Virtually all of them had selected some country outside of Southeast Asia, with Canada being their first choice as a place in which to study, followed by the United States, Japan, Australia, New Zealand, and England, approximately in that order. It is especially noteworthy that very few had designated either Nationalist or Communist China as a desirable place for advanced study.

A strong note of family loyalty and solidarity runs through many of the student expressions, both of confidence and of despair regarding their occupational prospects after graduation. It is as though the obligation to assist younger members of the family and to bring happiness to aging parents was an added incentive to greater determination to succeed or a basis of deeper despair at the prospect of failure.

> I must join the army for three years
> and afterwards I will get a job to help
> my family and to support my brothers
> in education. . . . Then I will get
> married. It is too early to predict how
> things will be, but I believe in this:
> my fate is in my own hands.--Commerce/2/M

> It would be ideal, if assisted by good
> fortune, I would be able to obtain a
> good job, for the wish to repay the debt
> of gratitude to one's parents is univer-
> sal. The children have the responsibility
> to support their aged parents and to re-
> lieve them of hard labour in their old

age.--Science/2/F

> I hold a pessimistic view regarding job
> prospects. Without a job, even though I
> won't suffer starvation, it is rather
> a hard life to bear under the reproach-
> ful, disappointed eyes of my family mem-
> bers. The worst is their notion that a
> university education is a "golden-coat,"
> which deserves a large investment, with
> the promise of fat returns. Should their
> expectation of my getting a well paid job
> after graduation be disappointed, the con-
> sequences are unimaginable.--Arts/1/F

Some concerns of this nature--for the way in which

personal achievements are viewed by family and

friends--is fairly normal among all college stu-

dents. What appears especially distinctive about

most Nanyang students is the intensity with which

this sense of family obligation affects their

lives, even though its influence is not formally

acknowledged. Indeed, one is led to suspect that

an occasional renunciation of responsibility for

one's family and the asserted desire of leading

"a wandering life" and of tasting "what hippies'

life is like" reflects an idle dream rather than

any serious intention.

As a final test of what the Nanyang students

were looking forward to in adult life, they were

asked to indicate the one country from a list of

thirteen possibilities in which they would prefer

to live. Obviously the answers to this sort of

question lie very much in the realm of conjecture

175

and cannot be regarded as more than an expression of present-day desire. Although the great majority (60 percent) of the students, as one would expect, indicated a preference for Singapore where they had been born and which was home to them, it is notable that the remaining 40 percent indicated a desire of breaking away, and that Switzerland should have exercised the strongest attraction (15 percent) of any foreign country.[18] Canada came second as the foreign country with the greatest appeal to 6.1 percent of the Nanyang students, while Communist China placed third, being preferred by only 5.9 percent. This relatively low figure is all the more significant in the light of the attraction which Chinese communism was alleged to have had for Nanyang students less than a decade earlier.

The very low appeal of Malaysia as the preferred place of residence—to only 4.4 percent of the students in the survey despite the fact that 13.2 percent of the student body come from Malaysia—reflects the deep-seated sense of being discriminated against which so many Chinese experience there and which was greatly intensified by the racial rioting during the summer of 1969. None of the other nine countries listed had been able to excite the special interest of as many as 3 percent

176

of the students, although Japan and Taiwan were each designated as the preferred country by 2.9 percent, greatly outranked the United States, Indonesia, Hongkong, or England, or France; Russia was not selected by a single person.

Notes

1. Donald and Joanna Moore, The First 150 Years of Singapore (Singapore, 1969), p. 474.

2. Quoted in Alex Josey, Lee Kuan Yew (Singapore, 1968), p. 449.

3. Ibid., p. 517.

4. No institutions of higher learning have thus far emerged in Singapore to accommodate graduates of the Tamil or Malay streams of education, despite the widespread use of both languages and the prevalence of both cultures in the surrounding region. Neither is there any likelihood that such institutions will develop in the forseeable future.

5. Alex Josey, op. cit., p. 66.

6. More than 90 percent of the total school population of Singapore in the late 1960s were enrolled in schools using both Chinese and English. Gwee Yee Hean, "Education and the Multi-Racial Society," in Ooi Jin-Bee and Chiang Hai Ding (editors), Modern Singapore (Singapore, 1969), p. 214.

7. Actually there was a noticeable drop in the total number of male students at Nanyang during the sixties--from 1,525 in 1961 to 1,362 in 1969--chiefly in the colleges of Arts and of Sciences and only partially counterbalanced by a significant rise in the College of Commerce.

8. If a correction were made for the fact that the Department of Economics had been transferred to the College of Commerce in the meantime, the comparable ratios for 1969 would be 51.6 percent

for the women and 39.0 percent for the men.

9. A considerable majority of Nanyang students in 1969 not only regarded Singapore as their home (84.7 percent), but nearly two-thirds (65.9 percent) of the students included in the survey had also been born there, the difference, of course, being a natural consequence of the continuing migration of families from Malaysia and Indonesia into the metropolitan center.

10. Only a scanty 3.0 percent of the students indicated that either their father or mother were still living in China, although for this small segment, the emotional ties to present-day China could be very great. It is probable also that most of the Nanyang students' families have close relatives still living in Communist China about whose welfare they are concerned, but no effort was made in this study to determine the nature or extent of these contacts.

11. As indicated earlier (page 43), the Cantonese are the one Chinese provincial group with a significant excess of females over males in the adult population of Singapore, whereas among all the other groups there has been the usual excess of males over females commonly found in any immigrant population. As a consequence, a considerable number of Nanyang students, whose mothers are Cantonese, have fathers of some other dialectal group, notably Hokkien and Hainanese.

12. Based on data from Singapore Sample Household Survey, 1966 (Singapore, 1967), p. 289. Unfortunately this figure refers only to the income of the single individual designated as the head of the household, whereas the data from the student survey take account of the shared income, derived from the earnings of a median of 1.2 persons per family.

13. This particular part of the survey was designed primarily to provide needed information for the administrative staff of the university, and much of it is not germane to the present study. There were, however, certain questions which shed light on student inclinations of a more fundamental nature, and these will be discussed in the subsequent pages.

14. For all quotations from student comments, the only identifying information is as follows: the college in which the student is enrolled, his year in college, and sex. All quotations of this type are taken from a 30 percent sample of representative questionnaires from all departments.

15. The selection of student comments to be included in the text is chiefly to illustrate the range and intensity of sentiment on the topic under discussion, and the number of quotations is, therefore, no indication of the extent to which comments were made.

16. A minor demonstration did occur on the Nanyang campus early in 1969, over "the cucumber incident," in which campus guards were alleged to have helped themselves without permission to cucumbers cultivated on the campus by students in botany.

17. John C. H. Wu, "Chinese Legal and Political Philosophy," in Charles A. Moore (editor), The Chinese Mind (Honolulu, 1967), p. 32. The notion that fatalism and pessimism are central and immutable elements of "the true man" is apparently deeply implanted in the traditional Chinese ethos.

18. This, no doubt, is chiefly a consequence of the public attention given to Switzerland as a model of a multicultural and multilinguistic community which Singapore might properly seek to emulate.

5

RACIAL AND ETHNIC PERSPECTIVES

Although the presence within the same community of
such sharply contrasted and virile cultures as those
of the Malays, Indians, Chinese, and Europeans has
long been recognized as a possible threat to the
peace and welfare of the whole of Southeast Asia,
the most notable tendency among administrators and
scholars alike has understandably been to deal with
the issue with as light a touch as possible in order
to avoid setting off its explosive potentials. In
his widely read background book entitled _Malaysia
and Singapore,_ K. G. Tregonning, Raffles Professor
of History at the University of Singapore, has summarized the existing situation as accurately as anyone, but one can immediately recognize the wariness
with which the subject has been approached.

> Race relations, because of the divergent
> cultures, is a matter of some apprehen-
> sion. It is often said that communalism,
> not communism or colonialism, is the
> major danger facing Malaysia, and in-
> deed it is very clear that harmonious
> relationships between the peoples is es-
> sential if the state is to survive.[1]

He goes on to say that although the potential danger is recognized, "interrelationships are courteous and smooth; racial prejudices, if felt, are a

personal thing and are scarcely ever a matter of issue." In commenting later on the long history of Singapore in which there had been considerable rioting especially by the Chinese against the government, the point is explicitly made that up to that time "there had never been a Sino-Malay riot. In nearly 150 years of history, with all the changes that had come, the two races had lived on the island side by side, and never once had fought each other."[2]

This relatively peaceful situation had prevailed under the segregative policy of British colonial rule when relationships across racial lines were kept at an essentially symbiotic level and where, as Tregonning points out, they "do not live and rarely work together . . . /but/ exist side by side, each necessary to the other but neither forced to surrender much of what he treasures."[3] Following Independence, however, and the subsequent struggle among the emerging interest groups for control over their own destinies, the inherent differences in values among them began to come into open conflict with one another, and the earlier peaceful relations were seriously threatened.

In the summer of 1964, less than five years after full internal self-government was established

in Singapore, bloody rioting between Chinese and
Malays broke out during the celebration of Mo-
hammed's birthday, in the course of which 22 persons were killed, some 450 persons were injured,
and 1,700 arrests were made before the disturbances
were brought under control. This particular tragedy
and others less violent which followed later that
year were in large part the culmination of the extended rivalry for political strength between the
Chinese-dominated PAP (Political Action Party)
under Lee Kuan Yew's leadership and the UMNA
(United Malays National Organization) of which Syed
Ja'afar Albar was the most active spokesman.[4]
Under the heightened emotional intensity of this
struggle, the shedding of blood was publicly urged,
presumably to counterbalance the alleged injus-
tices which Malays were experiencing under the
Singapore government. The exercise of close
police supervision and the adherence to a policy of
strict impartiality in the dispensation of justice
across racial lines has prevented a recurrence of
any incidents of comparable seriousness in Singapore, but the highly destructive and frenzied
rioting in Malaysia during 1969 served as a tragic
reminder of how vulnerable Singapore can also be to
explosions of this nature.

The common disposition of seeking to exorcise

182

a problem by disregarding or minimizing its significance is all too apparent in Malaysia's racial
experience throughout the period since Merdeka
(Independence), as, of course, it is also in other
parts of the world. There is at least a tacit
admission of this weakness in the Tunku's introduction to his interpretive volume on the May 13th
tragedy.

> Time and again during these years of
> independence since 1957 I have been
> asked as Prime Minister how I managed
> to keep the many races in this coun-
> try with their different customs,
> religions and ways of life so peace-
> ful and united. My reply was always
> that the answer lay in the nature of
> the people themselves, as all our
> component races are tolerant and
> friendly. Everyone is free to carry
> out his own interests in life, whether
> in business, in the professions, or in
> politics. As individuals or groups we
> might have our likes or dislikes and
> were at liberty to pursue them. We
> might agree or disagree, but always we
> worked together because we believed
> the spirit of democracy was the best
> medium of expression of our way of
> life.[5]

There had been a number of outbreaks of violence
over the years, primarily between Malays and Chinese, which had been recognized nationally, but
none of them involved nearly the same widespread
virulence as those of 1969. On 13 May of that
year, following a series of provocative incidents
associated with the general elections a few days
earlier, there was set in motion in the urban cen-

ters of Malaysia a succession of violent confrontations between Malays and Chinese and Indians, characterized five months later by the deputy and subsequently the Prime Minister as follows:

> May 13, 1939 will go down in our history as a day of national tragedy.
> On that day the very foundation of this Nation was shaken by racial disturbances whose violence far surpassed any we had known . . . . On that day we were jolted into a sharp realization that the racial problem in this country is a serious one and measures taken in the past to cope with it have not proved adequate.[6]

Although the casualties resulting from the racial violence between 13 May and 31 July 1969 were officially reported as 196 deaths, in addition to 39 missing persons and 439 persons injured,[7] it is commonly believed, especially in Singapore, that these figures were unduly conservative. Moreover, the rigorous means employed to censor all reporting of the news by the mass media and to outlaw as "rumor-mongering" any discussion of the emergency except in accordance with information released by the government, quite naturally led to the popular impression that conditions must have been far more serious than the administration was willing to admit. The accounts by foreign reporters, as long as they were permitted, gave support to the widespread impression that the Chinese were the principal victims of the rioting, both in loss

184

of life and of property, and this was clearly con-
firmed by the official statistics,[8] however in-
complete they might be.

Singapore was fortunately spared the direct
impact of this crisis, although the indirect re-
percussions were considerable, owing to the close
economic and familial ties between the two countries. Many of the residents of Singapore, including the students of Nanyang, suffered loss or
injury to members of their own families or close
relatives and the destruction of their homes or
sources of livelihood as a result of the Malaysian
holocaust, and many more remained for weeks in a
state of anxiety lest they experience a similar
fate. Some of the bitter feeling engendered by
the rioting and senseless killing in Malaysia did
spill over into Singapore in a series of encounters
between Malays and Chinese in which at least two
persons were killed, a score or more were hospitali-
zed, and some property was destroyed. In order to
hold such violence in check, the Singapore police
conducted a series of "scoops" or raids on areas
of the island in which racial tensions were high
and more than seven hundred persons were brought in
for questioning, weapons were confiscated, and
arrests were made on charges of "rumor-mongering"--
all of which undoubtedly served the intended pur-

pose but also contributed to the general anxiety in the community.

The racial conflagrations of 1969 were vivid reminders to many of the Chinese in both Malaysia and Singapore of the discriminatory legislation and treatment to which they or others of their race had been subjected in Indonesia under both the Dutch colonial and the independent native regimes. The expulsion of Chinese shopkeepers and merchants from all rural areas of Indonesia in 1960 and the consequent disruption of life for such a large part of the population stood out as a major harassment within the country itself, but the barrage of propaganda from Indonesia during the three years of the Confrontation (1963-1966), representing the Chinese as the subverters and exploiters of Malaysia probably contributed more to the racial tensions within Singapore, and this certainly figured prominently in the riots in 1964.

Chinese Reactions to Malays

Considering the intense excitement among all elements of the population throughout both Singapore and Malaysia following the May 13th incidents, the relative calm prevailing among the student body on the Nanyang campus throughout the ensuing weeks and months is truly remarkable since the lives and property of the families and relatives of so many

186

students were in jeopardy. This is all the more
notable in view of Nanyang's earlier reputation
for violent demonstrations over matters affecting
the students much less directly, including labor
unions and national politics, and a minor conflagration had developed on the campus earlier in the
same year over the theft of some cucumbers. Perhaps the very seriousness of the disturbances during
the midyear of 1969 and an awareness of the drastic
steps which the government was prepared to use in
suppressing any demonstrations in Singapore served
to discourage the expression of feelings which were
unquestionably there. Certainly the tensions between the Chinese and the Malays, especially in
Malaysia but also in Singapore, were the topics
of major discussion among the students in the dormitories, the canteens, and even in the classrooms
for many weeks, but there were no organized pro-
tests or mass demonstrations to come to the
attention of an outside observer.

On the theory that underneath the external
calm of the Nanyang students during this period
there must be a considerable body of undisclosed
but potentially significant feelings on racial matters in the region, it seemed desirable to try prob-
ing into these dispositions in conjunction with the
survey conducted on the campus just four months

187

after the outbreak of the Malaysian riots. Two of the 12 pages in the questionnaire were devoted to a rating of 21 racial or ethnic groups presumed to have entered into the experience of Nanyang students, either by direct face-to-face association or through the mass media. Each student was first asked to indicate how he would rate each of the groups as the source of his own marriage partner on a 5-point scale of acceptance--1. would gladly accept, 2. willing to accept, 3. indifferent, 4. would oppose, 5. would strongly oppose. It was assumed that marriage would be very much to the forefront in the minds of all the students as an immediate or more remote prospect after graduation, and that their deepest feelings, either of acceptance or rejection of such groups, might be elicited in answer to a question of this nature. Although an average of 12.5 percent of the students failed to respond to this part of the questionnaire for a variety of reasons, including the declared intention of some that they definitely would never marry,[9] the results from the other 87.5 percent do reveal a wide range and considerable depth of feeling.

In order to probe even deeper into the circumstances or conditions behind such quantitative expressions of feeling, the students were also asked

188

to indicate in writing the reasons they had for designating any of the groups either as highly acceptable or as highly objectionable. This particular approach would obviously call forth only the more extreme positions on the part of the students, but in the absence of more direct and personal contact with them by the researcher, this was as much as could reasonably be expected. As affecting future policy, it is, of course, these extreme and frequently irrational and unyielding positions which are of critical significance, and without some such unstructured and anonymous comments by the students, any valid interpretation of their statistical ratings of the racial and ethnic groups would have been difficult, if not impossible. Although the students were asked to make their evaluations of the groups and to explain them on a purely individual and personal basis, it soon became apparent-- as was expected--that they were in most instances reflecting sentiments prevailing in the families and communities of which they were a part.

What did indeed become apparent from both the statistical summaries and the written comments by the students was the depth of the opposition among Nanyang students to close association with Malays in marriage, and that although much of this adverse feeling had its roots in long-standing and fundamental cultural distinctions between Malays and Chinese, the sense of difference was significantly accentuated as a result of the 1969 riots. Not only was the adverse sentiment toward the Malays the highest of any group (76.6 percent), but the use of the designation of "strongly oppose" was likewise the highest (32.1 percent), while only 8.1 percent were disposed to admit any acceptance of them, while the remaining 15.3 percent refrained from expressing any opinion on this issue. Because the Malays and Indonesians are so similar to one another culturally and religiously, the Nanyang students tended to rate them very much alike and to apply much the same explanations for their objections to them as marriage partners. There is, of course, also common knowledge that the Chinese had been involved in earlier struggles just as bloody and devastating with Indonesians as with their cousins in Malaysia. Thus the Indonesians were rated as only slightly less objectionable as marriage mates than the Malays, with 74.3 percent of the students expressing some degree of opposition, and 28.6 percent indicating strong opposition.

Few, if any, of the Nanyang students had ever before been presented with a request to supply an explanation for a judgment which must have appeared to most of them as entirely self-evident, namely,

190

the transparent superiority of one's own way of life and the consequent disposition to avoid association with those who differed most markedly with it. Faced with such an ingenuous query, the natural tendency of many students was merely to fall back on the familiar stereotypes of the Malays and Indonesians which were so commonly repeated by their associates. Thus among the Chinese, whose conditions of life both in China and in Southeast Asia placed a high value on industry, initiative, and hard work, the Malays and Indonesians appeared to be "lazy," "pleasure loving," and "lacking in initiative and ambition," and, therefore, undesirable as marriage mates. Their unsuitability in close family relations was as frequently stated in more general terms as a consequence of differences in religion, language, and eating habits, such as the taboo on the eating pork. In many instances, no attempt was made to specify the bases of objection except to say, "their ways upset me very much," or "I just don't like them," or "I have an inbred abomination of them."

The more thoughtful responses by the students revealed the interplay of a variety of different considerations, with at least occasionally the mention of some compensating trait. One sees in the following statements the reflection of the con-

191

cerns that were uppermost in the minds of the students.

> I would strongly object to a Malay as my
> marriage partner, because they are lazy
> but lavish spenders. They are compara-
> tively uncultured and untrustworthy. In
> the recent riots Malays even slaughtered
> innocent school children and infants with-
> out a streak of mercy in them and taking
> the law into their own hands.--Arts/1/M

> Because almost all Malays are Muslims and
> their intelligence on the average is lower
> than among the Chinese. Persons with ex-
> tremely different religions would find it
> hard to live together.--Arts/2/F

> Because the Malays are not diligent, have
> dark skins and the majority of them attain
> a very low level of education.--Science/1/M

> I couldn't accept a Malay, an Indonesian, or
> a Filipino as my marriage mate simply be-
> cause of the differences in religion,
> language, and custom. Moreover, they lack
> mercy and justice, they are selfish, lazy,
> and dirty. The May 13th incidents in
> Kuala Lumpur and the anti-Chinese activi-
> ties in Indonesia and the Philippines make
> me disgusted with them.--Arts/2/F

The frequent reference, particularly by the women
students, to the strongly adverse sentiments toward
the Malays within their own family and kinship
groups suggest that their characterizations are
borrowed rather than the consequence of direct
personal experience. The allusions to the Muslim
religion, according to whose tenets any outsider
inclined toward marriage with a Malay would be required to embrace the religion of Islam, seem to
imply that this barrier automatically precludes

192

any possibility of reducing the social distances between the two races. Special mention was also made by the women students to the acceptance of polygamy among the Malays and the consequent inferior status of their sex.

Chinese Pride of Race and Ancestry

The testimony of the Nanyang students in the previous section seems to illustrate the familiar folk saying that "peace at home is increased by war abroad." Unquestionably the Chinese pride in their cultural heritage does frequently intensify the feelings of disgust or disapproval toward people whose customary ways of life run strikingly contrary to their own, but the statements by the students with reference to a number of the groups suggest just as frequently the presence of attitudes of either indifference or conditional acceptance. There can be, however, no doubt as to the overwhelming preference of the Chinese for members of their own racial ancestry, and, of course, it would have been strange if it were otherwise. British, Malay, or Indian students would certainly have responded to a greater or lesser degree in much the same way with respect to their own group.

Despite the existence of important ethnic distinctions within the Chinese community, of which the students were asked to take account, nearly

193

one-third of them (30.2 percent) simply indicated
their willingness to accept a person of any of the
five major subgroups, so long as he or she was of
Chinese ancestry, and none of these Chinese ethnic
groups was rejected by more than 14 percent of the
students as an acceptable source of a marriage mate.
This general readiness among the Nanyang students
to find their life partner almost without restric-
tion inside the Chinese community--averaging 63.4
percent--stands in sharp contrast with their very
low rate of acceptance of any group outside that
limit. Of the sixteen non-Chinese groups of whom
the Nanyang students were presumed to have had some
knowledge either by direct association or by reading, persons of only two--the Japanese and the
Vietnamese--were even thought of as possibilities
by as many as one-fifth of the students, and on the
average these outside groups would be considered
by no more than 13.5 percent, whereas even this
slight possibility was definitely rejected by an
average of 62.5 percent. The common disposition
was for students to rate each of the Chinese
ethnic groups as "acceptable," and all others as
unacceptable (see Table 8).

The bases for rejecting outmarriages of any
sort must not, however, be attributed wholly or
even primarily to ethnic or racial pride. The wide-

194

spread and understandable fear or aversion of the
unfamiliar might be interpreted as the obverse of
pride in the familiar, and this undoubtedly plays
a part in the students' reactions. But their
cited justifications for summarily rejecting the
idea of marriage outside the ancestral community
usually centered on the conflicts in cultures
and understanding that they assumed must follow
from such a venture, affecting not only the parties
most directly involved, but their relatives, as
well, and most markedly the children. Student
comments repeatedly emphasized that similarity of
language, moral and religious values and practices,
and styles of life would make the everyday problems
of living together much less difficult, and frequent
reference was made, on the other hand, to the
questionable status of the children of racially
mixed marriages and the discrimination and social
deprivation to which they are likely to be subjected. Comments such as the following were common.

> People with similar language naturally
> can communicate better and have greater
> emotional attachment which would prevent
> misunderstanding and conflict, for the
> happiness of a family lies in the mutual
> understanding and co-operativeness of
> each constituent member.--Science/2/F

The grounds cited by the students for welcom-
ing or at least accepting persons in the Chinese
community as potential marriage partners are, of

Table 8

Acceptability of Persons in Various Racial and Ethnic Groups
as Marriage Partners (in percent)

Racial and Ethnic Groups	Favorable to Acceptance	Indifferent	Opposed to Acceptance	Strongly Opposed to Acceptance*
Hokkiens	74.6	22.1	3.3	1.0
Teochews	71.4	24.7	3.9	1.3
Cantonese	62.5	29.9	7.6	1.7
Hakka	52.5	33.8	13.7	3.0
Hainanese	53.2	33.2	13.6	3.4
Japanese	38.9	27.3	33.7	9.3
Vietnamese	22.6	33.5	43.9	11.7
Siamese (Thai)	17.9	32.0	50.1	13.9
Eurasians	18.1	26.6	55.3	17.8
English	16.6	32.9	50.5	15.0
Italians	13.7	28.9	57.4	18.8
Americans	13.2	26.8	60.0	19.6

Table 8 (continued)

Racial and Ethnic Groups	Favorable to Acceptance	Indifferent	Opposed to Acceptance	Strongly Opposed to Acceptance*
Filipinos	10.5	25.8	63.7	21.8
Scandinavians	9.4	24.9	65.7	22.0
Russians	9.1	22.8	68.1	24.5
Jews	7.7	21.6	70.7	25.4
Indians	7.2	18.0	74.8	25.7
Pakistanis	6.2	18.3	75.5	25.3
Negroes	6.6	18.2	75.2	25.6
Indonesians	8.0	17.7	74.3	28.6
Malays	8.4	15.0	76.6	32.1

* Included in previous column.

course, quite frequently the obverse of those cited for rejecting the Malays or Indonesians in this relationship. Thus, similarity in language and customs and a resulting ease of communication with members of the student's family were mentioned repeatedly as the obvious and incontestable reasons for preferring a member of one's ingroup.

> I accept only a Chinese to be my marriage partner, because I am a Chinese, a one-hundred percent Chinese, and for no other reasons! After all, who would want a family row to turn into a racial conflict?--Science/2/M

> My family is the embodiment of the old traditions, highly conservative. There-fore, for a person of another race to become one of its members is completely out of the question.--Science/1/M

> I would gladly accept a Teochew as my life-partner because I must live to-gether with my parents after marriage. The members of my family and relatives will easily mingle with a Teochew girl because they have the same dialect. Therefore, atmosphere of the family will be more harmonious. But Cantonese or Hokkiens would be acceptable too.--Arts/1/M

> Interracial marriage brings along prejudice and scorn from relatives and friends. This would have an unhealthy effect on the young hearts of the future generation. Besides /with inter-racial marriage/ it is impossible to pre-serve the good traditions from the past. These pose serious problems to the couple who have yet to face the possible dangers of emotional alienation because of cul-tural and customary differences.--Arts/1/F

> To accept any race other than the Chinese would be contrary to our traditions and I would be discriminated against by my own race as well as by my wife's race. Be-

198

sides I am proud of my own culture and
customs, and I wouldn't want to accept
anyone else's culture, even though it
might be good. It is clear enough that
there is a big gap between my race and
other races. There is no harm in accepting them as friends or work-mates,
but never as a marriage partner.--Arts/2/M

Here, quite naturally, the positive stereotypes regarding the Chinese come into prominence, representing them as "diligent, industrious, thrifty, well-
mannered, generous, kindly, and cultured" and such
considerations operate strongly enough in many instances to rule out completely any thought of
marriage outside the favored race.

On the other hand, there was evidence, most
notably among students in the College of Arts, of
a sense that racial or ethnic exclusiveness might
be unworthy of cultured persons endowed with
Confucian jen (compassion, human heartedness).
Occasionally there were comments emphasizing the
duty of liberality and openmindness in human relations, although this might need to be tempered by
the primary obligation of filial piety and of
obedience to parental wishes, or personal considerations.

I would be willing to accept a person
from any of the groups, because they
are all human beings, and I have
nothing against them. The most important thing is that we both must
have the same religion and love for
each other.--Arts/2/F

Marriage within the race is an obvious practice, but one should adapt to the multi-racial condition of Singapore. One should be freed from the bond of obsolete prejudice against intermarriage as long as the marriage partner is of good character. But other things should be considered too in this matter, such as compatibility of habits, interests, religious and political beliefs, if the partner is to be of a different race.-- Science/Honors/M

I would accept any race as long as she is willing to become a member of my family.--Science/3/M

All races carry with them virtues and defects, but as a marriage partner is for a lifetime, the differences in living habits and customs which might influence married life ought to be taken into consideration. Therefore I give preference to people of the same race. This is not solely due to parental influence or objection. If I feel that intermarriage would bring happiness, I would try my best to convince my parents of the fact. I have no bias against any one race, and am willing to accept them as a marriage partner, and my family holds the same opinion excepting in marriage.--Arts/3/F

The Confucian dictum that "all people from the four corners of the sea are brothers," as one student suggested, applied more readily "if all the people are Chinese." The frequent citing of the politically approved proposition that "all races are equal" was almost as frequently followed by the mention of certain exceptional groups which were labeled as "narrow minded" or inferior in certain respects.

Along with the decided disposition of Nanyang

200

students to prefer persons of their own racial background in the more intimate relations of marriage, some recognition must also be given to their tendency to distinguish within the Chinese community on ethnic lines. It is only natural that, insofar as distinctive customary practices, institutional affiliations, or moral values still persist among the several Chinese subcultures, Hokkien would seek Hokkien in marriage, Hakka would choose Hakka, and similarly with each of the other ethnic groups. Thus, with only one notable exception, the overall rates of marriage acceptability within the Chinese community, as indicated in Table 8, correspond closely with the size of the ethnic group in the Nanyang student body, with the Hokkiens, as the largest group, showing the highest acceptability and the lowest rate of rejection. The Hakka group, on the other hand, having the smallest representation, received also the lowest rating of acceptance, although this was still very much higher than the positive rating received by any non-Chinese group. All five of the Chinese ethnic groups were rated as definitely unacceptable by some of the students, notably more so in the case of the Hakka and the Hainanese than of any of the other cultural subgroups, but the highest rate of rejection of 13.6 percent was still less than one-half of the lowest rate of rejection toward any non-Chinese group. A further sub-classification reveals that each ethnic subgroup, irrespective of sex, designated its own group as most desirable from which to draw a marriage partner.

Much the same positive stereotypes were used to justify the selection of a person of one's own ethnic subgroup as were used by other students to explain their designation of anyone of Chinese ancestry. Thus a Hakka student declares, "the Hakka are hard-working, diligent, simple, and thrifty," a Teochew describes his own group as "strict in discipline, but kind and considerate, genial in temperament, and courteous in manner," a Hokkien credits his group with "generosity, kindness, and open-mindedness," while others simply state that "similar language and customs make it easier to get along with me and my family." One notable variation was the tendency of some stu-dents--men to a greater degree than women--to select one or more of the Chinese ethnic groups, in addition to their own, from which to obtain a marriage partner. While usually recognizing the superior qualities of their own group, they would designate one or more other groups as possessing characteristics to which they were especially attracted, frequently on a romantic basis

202

I would gladly accept a Hokkien as my
life partner, because I am a Hokkien, and
I prefer them mainly because of our common dialect and customs which would help
us to understand and appreciate each
other. But I would gladly accept a Hainanese as my marriage partner because my
most intimate boy friend is a Hainanese.--
Arts/1/F

I would accept Hokkien and Teochew as
most acceptable because I am Hokkien and
my girl friend is a Teochew.--Arts/3/M

Hainanese girls are thrifty, hardworking,
and they make good mothers, and since I
am Hainanese, they would certainly be
highly acceptable, but Teochew girls are
tender, beautiful, and sophisticated.--
Arts/2/M

My target of marriage mates will be
among Teochew, Hokkien, and Hainanese
as I have frequently made contacts with
them, and I understand them more than
other races.--Arts/3/M Cantonese

My fiance is a Hakka.--Arts/3/F Hokkien

Since I am a Teochew, I understand them
best and there will be no difficulty in
my accepting one of them as a marriage
mate. But in my daily life, I have
contact with Hakkas very frequently and
I realize they are hardworking and
industrious and I would gladly accept
one of them as my partner.--Science/1/M

I would be happy to have a Hokkien because most of their women are tender and
obedient, a Teochew as they are beautiful, or a Hainanese who are hospitable
and friendly; besides they are all
Chinese.--Science/2/M Hainanese

I would prefer a Cantonese or Hokkien
wife, since I am a Cantonese and the
pattern of my life would be similar to
hers, and marrying a Hokkien is in-
expensive for after marriage there are
no festivities for the parents-in-law.
It saves a lot.--Science/1/M

Owing to the generally favorable disposition
of the five major ethnic groups within the Chinese community toward one another, there were
relatively few deprecatory stereotypes which
appeared in the student comments regarding any
of these groups. An occasional reference would be
made to one group or another as being allegedly
"stingy and cunning," "wild mannered," "calculating,
narrow-minded, ungrateful," or "difficult to get
along with." Among students with strongly anti-
Western sentiments, specific mention might be made
that "anglicized Chinese" were definitely ex-
cluded from the acceptable circle, but such comments
were decidedly infrequent. The strongly adverse
comments regarding other Chinese ethnic groups
which did appear may reflect the distinct affinity
and consequent competition and conflict between the
groups involved. As also might be expected, in
their rating of one another as marriage prospects,
the men students manifested a significantly greater
readiness than the women to obtain their partners
from outside their own ethnic group, whether from
one of the Chinese subgroups or not, but a
partiality toward their own group was clearly
evident among both men and women. It is worth
noting that of the small sample of eight students
who mentioned that they were either married or

engaged, six stated that their partners were of a different Chinese ethnic group from their own.

The relatively high proportion of Nanyang students who indicated their unwillingness to accept a Hakka or a Hainanese as a marriage mate undoubtedly reflects a widespread prejudice in the Chinese communities of Southeast Asia, growing out of a sense that these two groups, although surely Chinese, do not belong to the same extent that the others do. The adverse sentiments toward the Hakka were intensified by their having come originally as refugees from the north and their consequent segregation several centuries ago in the mountainous and less desirable areas of Fukien and Kwantung, while in the case of the Hainanese the discrimination grows partly out of the common assumption that they "have a good deal of aboriginal blood in their veins."[10] These traditional barriers have, of course, been reenforced by differences in language and customary practices which have existed from the outset or have developed over the intervening years.

Racial Distances--Great and Small

Between the two extremes of rejection of the Malays and Indonesians, on the one hand, and ready acceptance of the Chinese in their several subgroups, on the other hand, there is a very marked spread

205

in the depth of feeling expressed by the Nanyang students, as already indicated. Although there is no absolute consensus on either of these extremes, virtually all of the students take for granted the acceptability of persons of their own racial group within the intimacy of the family, even though they might be disposed to exclude one or more of the ethnic subgroups. The adverse feelings toward the Malays and Indonesians undoubtedly carry stronger emotional overtones, as reflected in the student comments, than those toward any other of the racial groups, although the statistical evidence, as reflected in Table 8, has been tempered somewhat by the growing sense in Singapore that such sentiments are either inappropriate or should not be expressed.

It might seem paradoxical, on first consideration, that the racial groups with whom the Chinese in Singapore and Malaysia have probably had the closest and most extensive dealings should encounter the greatest resistance from them as prospective family associates. On the basis of the statistical rating in Table 8, it would appear that the Indians and Pakistanis were almost on a par with the Malays and Indonesians in terms of acceptability as marriage mates, but the written comments were somewhat less vigorous by way of criticism, and the proportion of the students indicating very strong objection to them was significantly less--between 25.3 and 25.7 percent toward Indians and Pakistanis as compared to 32.1 percent toward Malays and 28.6 percent toward Indonesians. The written comments regarding the Indians and Pakistanis took the form generally of brief derogatory stereotypes such as "crafty, dirty, cunning, selfish, possessing unpleasant odour, dark-skinned," along with references to the Muslim religion of the Pakistanis and the "strange practices" of the Indians. These observations suggest that, although their homes might have been in close proximity to those of Indians or Pakistanis and they or their parents might have had business dealings with them, the contacts at a social or personal level had probably been meager or unpleasant.

> I am strongly opposed to either Malays or Indians as my marriage partners for the reason that Malays are lazy and indulge too much in impractical things, while Indians are dirty, talkative and lack a sense of mutual understanding. I dislike Indians more than Malays, chiefly I guess because of an Indian next-door neighbor, a boy who has been hanging around our place and who disturbs me in my study.--Arts/2/F

> The Indians are greedy, who would sacrifice everything for a small profit, short-sighted, and they make the worst coloured "large nation" in Asia.--Arts/3/M

207

There may have been close physical contact with Indians for both these and numerous other observers like them, but there is little evidence of communication of a sort likely to lead to association in marriage. Despite the overwhelming weight of evidence as to the depth of feeling which separates the Nanyang students from the likelihood of marriage with their fellow citizens of Indian or Pakistani ancestry, however, it is worth noting that 85, or, 7.6 percent, out of a total of 1,118 students who registered their sentiments on the issue, indicated a willingness to consider such a possibility.

The reaction of Nanyang students to Negroes as possible marriage mates represents in some respects a sharp contrast to their response to the Indians and Pakistanis, since direct association with Negroes had been very limited in any part of Southeast Asia and the students' acquaintance with them had been almost entirely through the literature and by the mass media. On the basis of the questionable information likely to be obtained from such sources, however, the adverse sentiments reflected in the statistics were as pronounced as toward any of the groups listed.

Judging by the written comments, it was primarily a reaction to the unknown and therefore dangerous which figured most prominently in their responses, and the color black was used to symbolize this barrier. It is, of course, impossible to determine on the basis of these data from what source this negativism toward a dark color may have developed, but of its existence among a large portion of the Nanyang students there can be no doubt. In most cases there was simply a laconic comment, "too black," "very dark," or "dark-skinned," with perhaps an added negative stereo-typed phrase, such as "simple-minded" or "primi-tive," testifying to the absence of any direct association or first-hand acquaintance with Negroes and a summary rejection of the unfamiliar. Even where the explanatory statements were somewhat longer, there was no evidence of a personal en-counter or interaction.

> I wouldn't accept a Negro because they
> are too dark and I wouldn't like to
> have children with pigmentation too
> different from mine. I can't appre-
> ciate their hair-form and the disparity
> in habits and ways of life is too
> great.--Commerce/2/F

> They look so dreadful, we can only see
> their white teeth and nothing else.--
> Commerce/2/M

Even in the very small number of students--74 out of a total of 1,114, or 6.6 percent--who expressed at least a willingness to consider the idea of marriage with a Negro, and who insisted that "black

is lovely" or that they were "sympathetic toward
their situation," one suspects that the sentiments
did not penetrate very deeply.

Although color was mentioned frequently as a
major or the single factor affecting the disposition
of the students toward non-Chinese groups with
reference to marriage, there is reason to believe
that it served rather more as a convenient
rationalization for other deep-seated feelings.
Certainly there is little correlation between
the skin color of the various groups and the degree
to which they were rated as acceptable or unacceptable, although this is not to disregard the
part which physical appearance, including the
shade of the skin, must have played in such
ratings by a group of impressionable young people.
As a negative factor, whatever strikes any of the
senses as unusually bizarre or unfamiliar could
have a frightening and repelling effect upon the
individual. It might be noted, in this connection,
that one student noted her objection to all whites
"because their whiteness has the look of dead skin
and their blue eye-pupils are overwhelming in blue-
ness as if they had disappeared," while others
simply stated that they detested all whites without
specifying whether or how much the color might be
a factor in their opposition.

210

Marriage and Imperialism

In the main, however, the professed objections to persons of the so-called white races were on different grounds than the color of their skin. Although the English, Italians, Americans, Scandinavians, and Russians receive somewhat similar ratings in an intermediate position on the scale, the written comments of the students made relatively little reference to their physical appearance, either as a repulsive or attractive feature. The English, who were judged statistically to be least objectionable among these five groups, appealed to some of the students as being comparatively "reasonable and understanding" and relatively easy to communicate with. On the other hand, there were more frequent expressed objections to them because of their association with the earlier colonial overlords of the region.

> The British are the manipulators of Asian peoples, and they are a race headed for universal condemnation if their social systems are not changed in time.--Arts/2/F

> The English are too shrewd and skilful in statecraft as reflected in their colonization.--Commerce/1/F

The relationship between British colonial practice and the suitability of English people as marriage mates is certainly obscure, but it was issues of this sort relating to national and international concern which figured most prominently in the student comments on the acceptability of the three larger European and American groups.

Thus the most persuasive argument against the consideration of either British or Americans seemed to be that their respective nations had been or were "imperialists and exploiters" of less powerful peoples, to which there might be added references to alleged objectionable traits of character.

> They (English and Americans) are imperialists and are having an undisciplined, indulgent, and soft way of life. Besides, they are abnormal in their way of thinking, having totally different cultures, customs, language from my own, and I don't think there would be any way of compromising those difficulties.--Arts/2/F

> The English display too strong an air of superiority and are too conscious about money matters. The chance of meeting with one virgin approaches nil. I am hostile towards the Americans and the Russians because of political reasons.--Science/1/M

The objections to the Russians and the Americans take on a considerably stronger tone, presumably because of the national opposition of their governments to China.

> The Americans are imperialists, being too unfriendly towards China and they have ambitions in Southeast Asia. Russia is an enemy of China, so naturally they can't be my friends.--Arts/1/F

> The Americans are hostile towards China.

212

> Besides they are capitalists, indul-
> ging in material comforts and are
> highly racist, as evident in their
> discrimination toward the Negroes.
> As to the Russians, their filth flows
> together with that of the Americans.--
> Commerce/1/F

> If I were to marry a Russian girl, what
> would happen if the Russians declared
> war on China? Obviously, we would be
> greatly hindered in our married life by
> a Russian-Chinese conflict.--Commerce/1/M

As the data in Table 8 indicate, the adverse feeling toward the Russians was considerably more pronounced than toward either the British or the Americans, and the written comments suggest that much of this additional antipathy is a reflection of the international scene. Statements repeatedly appeared in which the only adverse comments about the Russians was that "they are aggressive and never keep their treaties," "they are aggressive and expansionist," "brutal, the most dirty and bastard fellows in the world," "they are cunning, unscrupulous, selfish, and invasion-prone," "they are the bully-type who possess no record of good behaviour, cold-blooded murderers."

Critical comments relating to European and American character traits, both favorable as well as adverse, also appeared, but these were less clearly defined and more varied in scope and emphasis. In addition to the objections to the British and Americans, already noted, of their being "soft and

213

indulgent," it was claimed that both groups were "morally loose."

> People in Europe and America indulge too freely in abnormal social life. It is known that American girls are having better privileges than boys. They are shrews. How could I expect them to be tender?--Science/2/M

A number of students charged the Americans particularly with gross materialism and a consequent arrogance of spirit--"with raising their voice too much," "being haughty." On the other hand, an occasional student would comment, "One of my best friends is an American, he makes me love his country and people." There is also evidence that part of the higher rating which the Italians received as potential marriage mates as compared with Americans and Scandinavians was a consequence of manifesting--presumably with greater finesse-- traits regarded as objectionable in the latter. The Italians were credited by the men students with being "affectionate," "very artistic and romantic," "earnest and they always welcome you with open arms," "sophisticated," and "infatuating."[11]

Oriental Paradox

Student reactions to the Japanese present a somewhat similar anomaly. Certainly the treatment which the Chinese residents of Southeast Asia received at the hands of the Japanese conquerors

214

of the region was scarcely of the type which would encourage the development of the most intimate of all personal relations between members of the two groups. "As the long-time enemy of the Japanese, the Chinese were treated with brutality. Mass executions, large-scale financial extortion, cruelties without respite; these were the character-istics of the occupation."[12] Yet aside from the various Chinese subgroups, there was no set of persons more readily designated by the students of Nanyang as acceptable marriage mates and none less frequently rated as entirely unacceptable than the Japanese. The explanatory comments by the stu-dents provide a variety of clues to this curious paradox, although research at greater depth than was possible in this study would be required to resolve the mystery. As a single statement in-corporating the basic ideas of the male students who were favorably disposed toward the Japanese, the following is perhaps as representative as any.

> The Japanese belong to the yellow group;
> they have the same religion with me, and
> their culture and customs are very similar
> to the Chinese. Besides, Japanese girls
> are mild, well-mannered, and tender, and
> they love their husbands.--Science/2/M

Considering the relatively limited direct contacts which Nanyang students could have had with Japan-ese,[13] their impressions of them must have been

215

largely derived from the mass media, including the cinema and television, and this may partially explain the romantic cast in which so many of the ratings by the men were apparently made. The one descriptive term which appeared most frequently in the comments by the men students as applied to Japanese women--and for that matter to the women of any ethnic group which they rated highly-- was the word "tender," although other terms like "mild, well-mannered, affectionate, beautiful, and genial" also appeared repeatedly. Somewhat further of the flavor of such idealization of Japanese women, especially by the younger Nanyang students, is reflected in such statements as:

> The Japanese wives have become famous for their tenderness and geniality to their husbands. It would be like living in a fairy tale to have a Japanese wife.--Science/1/M

> Besides the fair skin they generally possess, they are beautiful, the taller the better. They are cultured, with a charming manner in dealing with people, and they are of commendable character. They are as good as Chinese, if not better.--Commerce/1/M

> The Japanese women are genial, tender, and know how to serve their husbands.-- Science/1/M

> Isn't the Japanese wife of one of our teaching staff beautiful? Besides they are close to us racially.--Arts/3/M

An assumed biological and cultural affinity between Chinese and Japanese was specifically men-

216

tioned by a number of the men students and was probably unconsciously operative in the reckoning of others. Reference was made to the fact that Japanese "are Oriental too, with a long history tracing back to Chinese influence," and that because of the linkage between the two peoples extending over centuries, "both are similar in culture and education and in their aspirant spirit." Somewhat this same consideration entered prominently into the relatively high rate of acceptance of Vietnamese and Siamese on the grounds that Chinese influence had largely penetrated these regions. The Vietnamese especially were rated as easy to get along with "because they have come under the strong influence of Chinese culture."

The existence of both biological and cultural bonds with Japanese, Vietnamese, and many of the people in Thailand did not, however, crowd out the memory of earlier tensions or conflicts, and among the third to a half of the Nanyang students who indicated that they were unwilling to consider marriage with persons of one or another of these three groups there were those who reacted chiefly on the basis of unpleasant incidents in which members of their family or friends had been involved.

> The Japanese invasion of China and Singapore lost me my family and I hate them.--
> Arts/1/F

> Innumerable innocent Chinese had died
> at their /Japanese/ hands.--Science/3/F

Probably few of the Nanyang students would react
as violently as the one whose statement follows, but
it is included to indicate how deeply these feelings
may run.

> I would never select a Japanese as a
> marriage partner, because they are by
> nature cruel, merciless, and relentless.
> This is true of every Japanese. They
> show no respect for the virtues of
> trust and a sense of shame. They adore
> autocracy; they abuse whatever power
> they have. Any nation or race which
> comes into contact with Japanese stands
> to lose, for they tend to take every
> chance to gain, even by employing supres-
> sion or swindle. This is evident in the
> invasion of China and Southeast Asia dur-
> ing the past century. Consider the crimes
> they have been guilty of in terms of the
> loss of life and property. A few years
> back a Chinese businessman in Singapore
> married a Japanese wife. The parents-in-
> law tried by all sorts of underhanded,
> vulgar means to swindle him of his wealth.
> He was finally driven out of Japan after
> he had lost all his wealth to the parents-
> in-law. This case serves to illustrate
> how cruel and inhumane the Japanese race
> is. How can we usher the wolf into our
> abode by marrying a Japanese partner?--
> Science/2/M

Fortunately reactions of such intensity are relatively infrequent among the students, since the
harsh realities of earlier days tend to become
softened with time, and ordinarily succeeding
generations do not react with the same bitterness
as those who initially experienced the tragic
encounters.

218

The mellowing influence of time on the more sensitive aspects of race relations is observable to a lesser degree in the rating given by the Nanyang students to the Filipinos. It is likely true that "historically, the greatest antipathy and open conflict in Southeast Asia between the Chinese and a host group occurs in the Philippines,"[14] as the evidence of repeated "systematic government-sponsored massacres" during the Spanish era, severe communal struggles during the American period, and continued discriminatory legislation under the republic seems to substantiate. Nevertheless, the Filipinos rate distinctly higher in the estimation of the Nanyang students as potential marriage mates than the Malays or Indonesians, with whom they are biologically related. One out of every ten students indicated at least a willingness to consider such a union, although the majority, of course, were opposed. Insofar as specific comments were made by way of explaining their reactions, primary mention was made of the discriminatory policy of the government of the Philippines toward the Chinese and the corresponding "unfriendliness and even cruelty" of most of the population.

> Being jealous of the economic strength of the Chinese, they adopt an anti-Chinese policy.--Commerce/1/F

> The government doesn't seem to be

The romantic inclination toward the Filipinos obviously plays some part in the favorable reaction
among the men students, but it is much less apparent
than toward the Japanese women. On the other hand,
the romantic dispositions of the Filipino men was
more frequently interpreted adversely as "loose
moral behaviours," as evidence of their "fallen
character."

     It might have been expected that the Eurasians,
by virtue of their presence in Singapore and Malaysia and their actual blood relationship with persons
of Chinese ancestry, would have merited as much
comment, either favorable or unfavorable, from the
Nanyang students as the Americans, Japanese, or
Russians, whose numbers and kinship relations in
the region were very much less, but this was
definitely not the case. Actually the Eurasians
occupied a place on the social-distance scale
(Table 8) similar to that of the Siamese and the
English and the frequency and the intensity of
feelings about them were much the same. Completely
contrasting myths with regard to the personal qualities of the Eurasians, by virtue of their mixed
biological heritage, prevail among the Nanyang
students--some insisting that they inherit "all

the good qualities of two or more races," while others, with equal assurance and no greater supporting evidence, repeat the commonplace stereotypes that their "racial impurity reflects biological impoverishment." The virtues of the Eurasians are stated in superlatives by the small minority (4.6 percent) who had been very favorably impressed, just as they were by the somewhat larger minority (17.8 percent) who vigorously opposed them as possible marriage mates.

> They /Eurasians/ possess more than a
> single racial character. Thus they
> are comparatively more nice-looking,
> charming, and tender than any of the
> other races.--Science/2/M

> Every race has its own points of
> excellence; the Eurasian has all the
> ingredients.--Commerce/1/M

> They /Eurasians/ are the embodiment
> of all the good qualities of two or
> more races and since they cut across
> racial lines, they bring greater
> racial harmony--most suitable for a
> multi-racial society like our own.--
> Commerce/1/M

> They possess the characteristics of
> all the races with a high I.Q. So,
> in order to propagate a young genera-
> tion of superior qualities, I would
> choose them as a marriage partner.
> For instance, in Southeast Asia, we
> have more talented Eurasians than of
> any other race.--Science/1/M

It is quite likely that a significant factor in the relatively high rating received by the Eurasians was their having such a large percentage of Chi-

nese blood, although the fact of its being di-
luted by an equal amount of European blood was also
the basis of much of the strong prejudice against
them.

Thus, in addition to the implicit assumption
in virtually all of the student responses that anyone departing from their own group norms by outmarriage would be subjected to discrimination,
there was also an adverse reaction among some to
the peculiarly anomalous status of the Eurasians
in Singapore and Malaysia. In a region where
multiracialism implies the retention of strong
racial ties, the Eurasians, so it was argued,
lack the distinctive cultural traditions necessary
for group pride and survival. Since they are
deprived of a sense of a history of their own,
they have no unique cultural heritage on which to
build. This was probably the basis for the frequent objection to the Eurasians as "not pure in
blood," or not knowing "who they are."

The Prospects in Race Relations

The questions as to the meaning of the foregoing
data as affecting the issues mentioned at the beginning of this chapter may still remain un-
answered to a considerable degree. There is ample
reason to doubt that the explanations offered by
the students for their rating of the various racial

222

and ethnic groups were in many instances little more than the expressions of stereotyped attitudes prevalent among the family, neighborhood, and peer groups of which they were a part. But the very absence and inadequacy of closely reasoned judgments and rationalizations for the choices is perhaps the best guarantee of their authenticity as expressions of deep-seated feelings and prejudices. Certainly the preponderant preference shown for all of the five Chinese ethnic groups and the equally vigorous rejection of all of the sixteen non-Chinese groups reflects the clear persistence of communal dispositions, not only within the Nanyang student body, but also within the communities from which the students come and to which they will presumably return. The overwhelming degree to which the Chinese in both Singapore and Malaysia do select their marriage partners within their own racial communities confirms this impression.[15]

The vigor with which many of the Nanyang students expressed their rejection of any non-Chinese marriage selection reflects assuredly a strong distaste for the ways of life among these outside groups and a corresponding disposition to keep them at a distance, but evidence from this and other sources (chapter 6) does not suggest any disposition to use violence or external pressure to maintain this distance. The reactions of the Nanyang students seem to substantiate Tregonning's contention, at least at the university level on the Chinese side, that "inter-relationships are courteous and smooth," as long as the appropriate distances are maintained. The widespread extent to which the Nanyang students concurred in these same dispositions, however, would throw into question the proposition that "racial prejudices, if felt, are a personal thing and are scarcely ever a matter of issue." The expressions of distaste are too much alike and they recur too frequently among the students to be merely personal. The strength of the adverse sentiments, especially toward the groups which reside in considerable numbers in the same communities with the Chinese, is such that relatively minor points of conflict could erupt into conflagrations of community-wide proportions. This has happened in Singapore in the relatively recent past, as for example in the 1964 episode and the 1969 disturbances in connection with the Malaysian riots, and it could happen again in spite of the precautionary measures of the government and the multiracial sentiments encouraged in the community.

One interesting and socially significant aspect of the ethnocentric dispositions of the Nan-

224

yang students with respect to marriage, not sufficiently recognized thus far in this account, is
the markedly greater tendency to favor the ingroup
on the part of the women than the men. Toward all
sixteen of the non-Chinese groups rated by the students, the men were consistently more tolerant and
accepting than the women, and this was also true,
although to a frequently insignificant degree, in
the case of the ethnic groups within the Chinese
community. This difference between the two sexes
was most apparent in the attitudes expressed toward
the Japanese, where the romantic inclinations of
the men seemed to come into full play, and the sex
differences were least evident in the dispositions
toward the Hokkiens, Teochews, and Cantonese.

The greater sensitivity on the part of women
than of men to the expectations of their family
and communal associates is probably the major
factor underlying the sex difference in the ratings.
The women, to a greater degree than the men, mentioned in their written comments the importance of
taking the family and community into account in
marriage selection and of seeking the happiness and
welfare of parents and relatives, although these
were also major considerations among the men despite
the less frequent reference to them in the written
accounts. It seems likely also that the boys and

young men had been culturally encouraged or at least permitted to be more venturesome in their associations than their sisters, and this probably led to a somewhat greater tendency to express approval of outmarriage than could be expected to be reflected in their own subsequent behavior. Although neither Chinese men nor women in Singapore marry non-Chinese to any marked degree, it is the women who do so to the greater extent--roughly four times as frequently as the men. Thus, although the Chinese women express themselves more conservatively than the men in matters of marriage and the family, they are probably also the more realistic of the two sexes in that their conduct more nearly corresponds with their profession.

In conclusion, there is perhaps need to be reminded that the data in this chapter are drawn almost wholly from the reactions of the Nanyang students shortly after one of the most devastating racial conflagrations in the history of Southeast Asia. Although the overt manifestations of the Malaysian explosions were relatively subdued in Singapore, the sense of their harrowing effect on the families and relatives must certainly have penetrated very deeply into the consciousness of the Nanyang students and intensified their normal wariness of outsiders in all their dealings. This

226

distrust of peoples whose speech, modes of living and thinking, and entire demeanor differed so strikingly from their own as the major racial and ethnic groups known in Singapore was all the more accentuated insofar as association with them was suggested at the most intimate level of marriage and the family. The heightened resentment toward the Malays growing out of the May 13th incidents could also be expected to magnify the students' sense of distance from all outsiders and to re-enforce their desire for the security among those they had always known.

Neither should the strongly derogatory comments used by some of the students necessarily be taken at face value as reflecting their disposition to act in accordance with those expressions. The fact of their having been asked to consider a possibility so remote from their normal disposi-tions as marriage with a Malay or Negro doubtless led some of them to reject the idea of close family relations with any non-Chinese group as utterly inconceivable. This did not necessarily imply, however, the rejection of association with any or all of the outgroups at other levels, such as work-mates, in trading relations, or as neighbors. All of the students, except for a very small minority (5.6 percent), reported that their families had some neighbors of racial groups other than their own, with whom they presumably lived in reasonable accord, and although Chinese were reported as the predominant group in the neighborhoods where 93 percent of the students lived, the remaining 7 percent of the students came from neighborhoods consisting chiefly of non-Chinese--3.1 percent of Malays or Indonesians, 1.5 percent of Indians or Pakistanis, and 2.4 percent of Europeans or Eurasians.

An interesting sidelight on the dispositions of the students toward non-Chinese racial groups is provided in their recording of what they believed to be the groups resident in Singapore which members of their family "least desired as neighbors." Insofar as the students felt capable of designating any single group as being held in such disfavor by their family, the ranking order of the various outgroups was much as it was as potential marriage mates for the students. The Malays and Indonesians were designated as least desirable as neighbors by 56.5 percent of these students, the Indians and Pakistanis by 15.0 percent, the Europeans by 5.7 percent, and the Eurasians by 3.3 percent.[16] Equally significant, however, was the reference by 19.6 percent of the students to one or another of the Chinese ethnic groups as least desirable as neighbors, ranked in the following order from most-to-least undesirable: Hakka, Hainanese, Cantonese, Hokkien, and Teochew.[17]

Finally, attention should be directed to the fact that despite the strong communal tradition which has been popularly accepted, if not extolled, throughout Singapore's history--notably so at Nanyang University during the earlier years of its existence--Chinese students were by no means unanimous in their readiness to accept a Chinese as their marriage partner. On the other hand, roughly one-third of the students manifested a favorable disposition toward one or more of the non-Chinese groups, and a small, but significant minority (4.3 percent) of the students indicated that both they and their families had their friendliest relations in the home community with persons who were non-Chinese, notably with Malays, but including Indians, Europeans, and Eurasians.

It is obviously impossible to predict whether the small minority among the Nanyang students and their families who have thus far bridged some of the cultural and temperamental distances separating the major racial groups in Singapore and Malaysia will soon increase or not. Despite the seemingly unyielding prescriptions on interracial fusion imposed by religious tabus and cultural pride, the very circumstances of life in a large metropolis such as Singapore are bound to force people of diverse backgrounds into some degree of contact with one another, superficial and fleeting though much of it may be. The mere fact of living in close proximity in nonsegregated neighborhoods over extended periods of time seems destined to wear away some of the stereotyped misconceptions which obstruct normal contacts across racial and ethnic lines. Gradually increasing numbers of persons will discover that behind their external differences of speech, dress, and modes of worship or of conduct, the Chinese, Indians, Malays, Europeans, and Eurasians still have their more important qualities of human nature in common. Some of the elements in the situation among the students of Nanyang University likely to influence the extent of such discoveries will be examined in the concluding chapter.

Notes

1. K. G. Tregonning, *Malaysia and Singapore* (Singapore, 1967), pp. 10-11. There is no evidence that in this context the author intends to refer any less to Singapore than to the rest of Malaysia.

2. *Ibid.*, p. 106.

3. *Ibid.*, p. 11.

4. James W. Gould, *The United States and Malaysia*

(Cambridge, 1969), p. 133.

5. Tunku Abdul Rahman, _May 13: Before and After_
    (Kuala Lumpur, September 1969), p. 4.

6. Tun Abdul Razak, _The May 13 Tragedy: A Report
    of the National Operations Council_ (Kuala
    Lumpur, October 1969), p. iii.

7. _Ibid._, pp. 88-96.

8. Of the 235 dead or missing persons reported
    by the Malaysian police at the end of July
    1969, 168 were Chinese, 32 were Malays, 20
    were Indians, and the remaining 15 were un-
    identified and classified as others. _Ibid._

9. Not all those who indicated a lack of interest
    in marriage were as frank as the Commerce
    College freshman who wrote, "I object to any-
    one becoming my life partner for I think all
    men are selfish and not trustworthy."

10. Victor Purcell, _The Chinese in Malaya_ (London,
    1967), p. 214.

11. Regarding the Scandinavians, there was a
    minimum of comments, most of which focused
    on the students' lack of experience with or
    knowledge about them and consequently ex-
    plaining their disapproval of them as poten-
    tial marriage mates. Much the same situation
    existed with reference to the Jews, although
    some of the commonplace stereotypes were em-
    ployed to bolster their low rating.

12. K. G. Tregonning, _op. cit._, p. 29.

13. No official data were available as to the
    number of Japanese residing in Singapore or
    Malaysia at the time of this study, but as
    recently as 1957 (the most recent date for
    which such data were available) there were
    less than 200 in Singapore.

14. George Weightman, "The Philippine-Chinese
    Image of the Filipino," _Pacific Affairs,_ 40
    (Winter, 1967), p. 315.

15. An unpublished study by Dr. Riaz Hassan, so-
    ciologist of the University of Singapore,
    indicates that only .68 percent of the grooms
    and a mere 3.12 percent of the brides among

the Chinese obtained spouses outside their own racial group during the seven years, 1962–1968. This is in sharp contrast with the situation in Hawaii, where during the same period of time, 59.5 percent of the grooms and 62.6 percent of the brides of Chinese ancestry found partners of non-Chinese ancestry.

16. Slightly more than a third of the students evidently felt incapable of answering this question and the foregoing percentages are, therefore, based on the responses of the other two-thirds.

17. The reaction of the students themselves to a question as to the groups with which they least enjoyed being associated reflected a ranking of both the Chinese and the non-Chinese in virtually the same order and degree as that of the family to these groups as neighbors.

6

NANYANG PERSPECTIVES

Most of the concerns of Nanyang University and of
its students discussed thus far in this study have
been colored to a greater or lesser degree by
considerations of their bearing upon the part that
persons of Chinese ancestry can or should play with
reference to the other racial groups in Southeast
Asia. In spite of the overwhelming predominance
of Chinese in Singapore or the possibility of
physical isolation in Chinese ghettoes in almost
any part of the region, the presence not too far
away of even larger numbers of people with differing appearances, aims, and objectives cast
their shadow, however slight, upon even such personal issues as the choice of an occupation, a
wife, or a place to live.

Under the conditions which existed during the
colonial period and during most of the interval
since Independence, it has been possible for the
Chinese in both Singapore and Malaysia to conduct
their life within the family and the close neighborhood very much as if the outsiders did not
exist, or at least as if they did not count except perhaps in the impersonal relations of trade.

Within the recent past, however, as reflected in the preceding chapter, points of tension across racial lines have become all too evident at certain critical junctures, and the evidence points to the increase in the frequency, if not of the intensity, of such outbreaks in the future.

Increasingly during the period of Independence, governmental agencies in Singapore have sought to develop a realistic outlook toward the peculiar problems resulting from the multiracial character of its people, and the future peace and welfare of the nation depends to no small degree on the success or failure of these efforts. The manner in which students at Nanyang react to the major issues of multiracialism, whether in support, indifference, or opposition, should shed significant light on the prospects in this regard, insofar as these young men and women occupy the vital positions in the life of the community that one might expect.

Without assuming that their attitudes and behavior as university students afford any sure guarantee of conduct in the adult community, it nevertheless seemed desirable to obtain from the Nanyang students, in conjunction with the 1969 survey, some clues as to how they stood on certain of the publicly announced policies with regard to multiracialism. So, among other things, the

234

students were asked to indicate on a five-point scale, from strong approval to vigorous disapproval, their reaction to sixteen different statements which had "appeared in published form or in private conversation regarding certain aspects of contemporary life." They were also asked to indicate the topics most frequently discussed with their fellow students, as a means of ascertaining the extent to which topics of this sort figured prominently in their casual and informal conversations. Probably even greater insight might have been derived from the comments of the students on these statements and topics, but unfortunately it did not seem feasible to place such an additional claim upon their time and willingness to cooperate.

Nanyang Interest in National and World Affairs

The physical location of Nanyang University, on an abandoned rubber plantation fifteen miles out from the center of Singapore, is interpreted by some observers as prima facie evidence of a desire by the founders, faculty, and students to perpetuate the distinctive culture and identity of the Chinese by isolating themselves from the main currents of life in the outside world. The classical Chinese style of the architecture in the impressive administration building and of the formal gardens which greet the visitors arriving on the campus

235

seem to confirm the impression of racial and cultural exclusiveness, and the well-nigh universal employment of Mandarin for purposes of communication on the campus has, in the not too distant past, added further support to the sense of Nanyang University's being and wishing to be a world apart. However valid such an interpretation may have been during the earlier years of Nanyang's history, the data from the 1969 survey indicate that a different and more cosmopolitan temper among the students has begun to develop.

Although two-thirds (66.8 percent) of the students rated "the opportunities of learning about the problems of the world" on the Nanyang campus as either somewhat or very unsatisfactory, and only 7.4 percent referred to them as satisfactory, this heavily negative reaction implies at least that such concerns are a legitimate area of interest. The relatively small proportion of the students who added any comments on this aspect of the official university activities explained the situation as a consequence of either the heavy demands on their time from technical courses or the indifference on the part of their fellow students.

> Most of the time we are so engrossed in lessons that we could not find time for even reading the newspapers, and there is no allusion to the news during the lectures. . . . Some students show a strong

apathy toward this matter.--Commerce/2/M

The more common references were made to the impressions that "Nantah seems insulated from society
at large," that "too little leisure, compounded
by too few interested students, results in no
opportunity," and that "the hope to score $\sqrt{\text{in}}$
courses$\sqrt{}$ seems to be of greater importance than
to learn about the problems of the world."

What is unquestionably much more impressive
with regard to a civic and international outlook
among Nanyang students is the extent to which such
concerns figured in the casual "talk-fests or bull-
sessions" on or off the campus. Although by no
means the most important or most frequently mentioned topic, it is significant that 21.1 percent
of the sample of 400 students whose written comments
were sampled, spontaneously selected world or international problems in their list of the five
subjects which were discussed most frequently with
their fellow students. A considerably higher proportion of the sample (37.0 percent) specified
topics relating more directly to Singapore or the
region of Southeast Asia under such general categories as national or current affairs, Singapore-
Malaysian relations, race relations, governmental
policies and practices, modernization, national
service, Singapore's future as a nation, and social

237

problems. Quite understandably, topics of a more
personal nature relating to career and employment
prospects, romantic interests and relations with
the opposite sex, the politics of campus life,
personal rivalries, and campus concerns and gossip
played a far larger part in the aggregate student
interchange.

The expressions of concern by many of the
students regarding their physical isolation so
far from the center of life in Singapore and what
they conceived to be the low level of interest
among many of their classmates are evidence of
a growing awareness of their civic responsibilities
at the local and worldwide level. References to
their "ivory-towered" existence on the hills back
of Jurong were frequently associated with recommendations that "more forums and discussions on
world problems should be organized" on the campus
and that more speakers of national and international
renown should be provided for student audiences.

> The interest in world problems among
> the students should be encouraged for too
> many of them are living in a sense in an
> ivory tower.--Arts/2/F

Students, especially in the social sciences,
lamented the fact that the supply of books in the
library dealing with world affairs and of news
journals and newspapers seemed inadequate. A

238

first-year student probably reflected the prevailing situation throughout much of the university
as one in which "we /students/ do discuss world
problems, but we find no place to raise our opinions." Comments by students in other fields
reveal that certain instructors seek to broaden
the perspective in class discussions to take account
of their national or international implications,
but this seemed to be the exception rather than the
rule. At the same time there were scattered inti-
mations that such discussions might not be entirely
healthy or safe--that "the walls might have un-
friendly ears," and that "anyone showing interest
in and concern for world problems runs the risk of
being 'black-listed' by government agencies on the
campus."

The period when Nantah was under severe fire
in the wider community as a suspected hotbed of
Chinese communism was too recent for the students
in the late nineteen-sixties to be unaware of its
continuing influence, and the responses to certain
items in the questionnaire unquestionably reflect
in part a sensitivity to their possible effect upon
them. Certainly the 1969 generation of Nanyang
students had full opportunity through the mass
media to become informed as to the existing points
of view in the community on the dominant issues

of the day, both those officially approved and those out of favor, but one would expect them to have been affected most profoundly by the definitions of the political party in power and most widely supported by the general public. A number of students implied what one of them definitely affirmed, that is, that the writings of "Karl Marx, Stalin, Lenin and Mao are dangerous topics for discussion, according to the statements of the government," and that it would be safest to express openly only the official version on other major critical issues.

Unquestionably the opinions of the students on the specific aspects of multiracialism discussed in this chapter have been colored to some extent by the pronouncements from official sources, of which some account needs to be taken. It would appear from the evidence, however, that, under the protective cloak of anonymity in the questionnaire, they were quite willing to express points of view at variance with those of the government.

Communalism versus Multiracialism

Whatever part purely political and personal rivalries may have played in the brief marital encounter between Singapore and Malaya, commencing in 1963 and ending abruptly in the separation of 1965, it is quite clear that the central issue on

240

which the merger broke down was the communal tension between the Malays and the Chinese,[1] and this soon assumed the form of an ideological struggle between communalism and multiracialism. Lee Kuan Yew's slogan of "Malaysian Malaysia" was clearly designed to symbolize a desired free and equal participation of all citizens regardless of their ethnic or racial ancestry, but it was interpreted rather as a threat and challenge to the special rights guaranteed to the Malays in the constitution and to the principle of political organization on the basis of racial ties. Although the effort to establish multiracialism as a basic policy failed in the Malaysian experiments of 1963-1965, it was possible for Lee Kuan Yew and his associates to secure sufficient popular support for making this a central precept in the formulation of the Constitution for the new Republic of Singapore, and he was able to speak confidently of the part he expected it to play in the entire life of the community:

> But whilst we have no control over events there /Malaysia/, independence has given us a unique opportunity to order our way of life, and I would like to believe that the two years we spent in Malaysia are years which will not be easily forgotten, years in which the people of migrant stock here--who are a majority--learnt of the terrors and the follies and the bitterness which is generated when one group tries to assert its dominance over

the other on the basis of one race, one
language, one religion. It is because
I am fortified by this that my colleagues and I were determined, as from
the moment of separation, that this
lesson will never be forgotton. So it
is that into the Constitution of the
Republic of Singapore will be built-in
safeguards in so far as the human mind
can devise means whereby the conglomera-
tion of numbers, of likeness--as a result of affinities of race or language
or culture--shall never work to the
detriment of those who, by the accident
of history, find themselves in minority
groups in Singapore. . . . We have a
vested interest in multi-racialism.[2]

Public statements reaffirming this point of view
have been made repeatedly by the Prime Minister
and his close associates in government during the
years following 1965, so frequently, in fact, that
the visiting observer, unfamiliar with the historical background, might conclude that the reference
to Singapore as "multiracial, multilingual, and
multireligious" was merely a hackneyed cliché.
There is ample evidence, however, that multiracialism, however broadly or loosely that term is
defined, has played a central role in the administrative practice.

A variety of different statements were incorporated in the Nanyang survey in an attempt
to determine whether such public pronouncements
had affected to any significant extent the dispositions and attitudes of the students. Most of
the statements bear at least tangentially on the

242

concept of multiracialism and the responses to
these affirmations probably reflect the attitudes
and dispositions, not only of the students themselves, but also to some degree of the families
and neighborhoods from which they come. It can
be assumed that since the survey was conducted
wholly on an anonymous basis, the temptation to
falsify or to "play up" to official expectations
would have been reduced to a minimum.

The reactions of the students to three of the
statements which focus directly on the idea of
multiracialism are summarized in Table 9.

Although the students indicated that they
were decidedly in agreement with the point of view
in all three of these statements, it is quite
apparent that the intensity of this positive judgment was distinctly less on the item in which the
Chinese were specifically mentioned. The abstract
principle of multiracialism, as specified in
statements 36 and 37, was much more readily and
almost unanimously agreed to than one which definitely disclaimed any dominance of the Chinese. It
is, of course, quite understandable that a somewhat
higher proportion of the students would either
express uncertainty or definite disagreement with
the idea of accepting multiracialism indefinitely,
but the most impressive aspect of this particular

243

Table 9

Agreement or Disagreement of Nanyang Students
with Statements on Multiracialism (in percent)

| Statement | Agree | | No Opinion | Disagree | |
	Very Strongly	On the Whole		On the Whole	Very Strongly
27. Singapore must never be thought of as a Chinese society, despite the fact that three-quarters of its residents are of Chinese ancestry.	36.8	37.8	11.6	9.3	4.5
36. All citizens should be permitted to retain their separate identity with respect to language, race, and religion as long as they respect these rights in others in accordance with the laws of the Republic.	62.9	27.5	6.4	2.3	0.9
37. A society which is multi-racial, multicultural, and multireligious must continue to be Singapore's goal for the indefinite future.	60.2	26.2	8.2	3.7	1.7

set of data is the relatively high degree of unanimity on the basic principle of multiracialism. There were no significant differences between the two sexes or among the different ethnic groups within the Chinese community in their acceptance of the idea of multiracialism but on this issue, as it related to the place of the Chinese, there was evidence of a slightly greater tendency toward ingroup sentiments among the students of Hokkien and Teochew ancestry than among those in the other three ancestral groups.

The crucial test of multiracialism, at least as conceived by the political leadership in Singapore, is the extent to which interaction occurs across race lines and a common means of communication emerges. Rather than encouraging the adoption by all the groups within a multiracial community of the language of the former colonial power, such as French, English, or Japanese, or of a single hybrid or trade language, the authorities in Singapore since Independence have given support to the retention and use of the several tongues among the major indigenous and immigrant groups in the region. This policy, of course, implies that either the various groups will remain unrelated and discrete or that a large proportion of the population must acquire, in addition to their own mother tongue, a facility in the language of the other groups. Singapore, with its economic dependence upon trade, has naturally chosen the latter course.

Very early in his career as Prime Minister of the newly independent state of Singapore, Lee Kuan Yew drew a sharp contrast between what he insisted was the segregative and exploitative policy of the former colonial regime and the democratic and participative approach of the one recently established. On 29 March 1960, in an address to the students of Nanyang University, Lee attributed the unfortunate situation in Singapore and Malaya "where nearly half of the population does not know what the other half says, writes or reads . . . /to/ the eagerness of the colonialists to exploit the national resources . . . by wholesale immigration of cheap labour."[3] It still seemed sensible to him at that time to expect the citizens of Singapore to "know Malay, the national language," and to work toward the time when "all speak one language and share common cultural values, although we are of different races and religions." Thus, he felt impelled to caution that although Chinese might continue to be the chief medium of instruction at Nanyang for "the immediate future . . . with every passing year

246

more and more of the national language must be taught and used, to keep in line with the trend of Malaya's linguistic future, and also to fit Nantah students to play a useful role in Malayan society."[4]

The disheartening experience during the two years of the Malaysian experiment, as well as the demographic realities in Singapore itself, however, evidently led Lee and his administrative colleagues to the conclusion that the earlier goal of one language (Malay) to be used by the entire population would have to be abandoned in favor of the principle of multilingualism. Financial support continued to be given by the government to private schools using as the medium of instruction any one of the four major languages--Malay, Chinese, English, or Tamil--and concern began to be expressed, even in official circles, for the preservation of enough of the ancestral cultures among the youth of the land to give them a sense of ethnic identity and "the will to succeed as a group." In speaking to the Nanyang students in October 1966, while still fully sensitive to the dangers of an overly chauvinistic or communal emphasis, the Prime Minister took major note of the equally "detrimental effects of de-culturation"--of producing "anaemic, uprooted floating citizens without . . . social

cohesiveness." He went on to state on another occasion at about the same time that the purpose of
the plan of education in Singapore with its four
major language streams was not to put the immigrant
children "through a sausage-machine, mince them
up, and make them come out in regular lengths at
the end of it."

> So, to each, what he originally
> had--his culture, his language, a
> link with his past, his heritage.
> And to each something added, so that
> they can meet and talk and under-
> stand . . . and eventually inte-
> grate into one society.[5]

Although the mode set by the Prime Minister
of becoming proficient in English, Mandarin, Hokkien, Cantonese, and Malay could hardly be followed by any number of Singaporeans, the goal of
providing every child in school with the ability
to communicate in at least one other language than
only his mother tongue was incorporated in the public education program of the republic. So also at
Nanyang, the ability to communicate in English
as well as in Mandarin has been a nominal requirement for some years, but owing to the
relatively inadequate skill in using the foreign
tongue on the part of many of the students, an additional requirement for graduation of two years
of English-language courses was imposed on all
students in 1969. The rationale for a multilingual

emphasis at Nanyang was succinctly stated by the
newly installed Vice Chancellor, Dr. Rayson Huang,
as follows:

> Realizing the role of science and
> technology in national development, the
> position in which Singapore is situated
> and the multi-racial character of our
> society, we have adopted a policy of
> making all our students bi-lingual. . . .
> Additional training is necessary to make
> them proficient in English, which is the
> world language of science, technology,
> and commerce in these parts. . . . Situ-
> ated where Singapore is, and composed as
> we are of peoples of different cultural
> origin, it only makes sense that all our
> citizens, not to mention those who have
> had a university education, should be
> at home in at least two languages and,
> if possible, three. Furthermore, steps
> are now being taken to make it possible
> for more students from the English stream
> of education to join Nanyang, beginning
> next year.[6]

The reaction of the Nanyang students to the
shifting and sometimes conflicting administrative
policies and ideology with respect to multilingualism in Singapore is partially reflected in
the responses to four statements in the questionnaire, summarized in Table 10. No single statement was directed specifically to the issue of
multilingualism, on the theory that the fundamental questions involved could be more fully
appreciated by the students and more effectively
explored through a reference to three of the four
major languages most widely used in the region.
Perhaps the most obvious finding from Table 10 is

249

Table 10

Concurrence of Nanyang Students with Statements
on the Use of Language (in percent)

| Statement | Agree | | No Opinion | Disagree | |
	Strongly	On the Whole		On the Whole	Strongly
40. Instruction at Nanyang should continue to be primarily in the Chinese language.	59.3	20.3	9.6	6.8	4.0
31. To be good citizens of Singapore, everyone should learn to speak Malay.	3.8	20.4	21.6	29.0	25.2
39. Malay ought to be Singapore's only national language.	3.5	9.6	15.6	23.0	48.0
32. To be good citizens of Singapore, everyone should learn to speak English.	5.2	24.2	21.1	27.6	21.9

the greater variation in the reactions of the students on the issue of the use of specific languages as compared with their opinions on the more abstract propositions of multiracialism.

The one question on which the students were in strong agreement was that Chinese ought to continue to be the principal medium of instruction at Nanyang. On all the other questions there was relatively little consensus, and the proportion who felt they could not express any opinion was relatively high. Nearly four-fifths of the students were agreed, on the other hand, that Chinese should be the principal medium of instruction at Nanyang, testifying both to their greater facility and ease in that language and probably also to their racial pride. It should be noted, however, that 10.8 percent of the students expressed their disagreement with this form of parochialism and thereby supported, by implication, a significant break with past traditions of the institution.

In the section of the survey which requested the students to list the major changes they would make at Nanyang "if you were the Vice-Chancellor," an occasional student would note that "the medium of instruction should not be limited to Mandarin alone," but the great majority of those who mentioned the use of the Chinese language at all in this connection were disposed to strengthen its role. Some students merely stated that Mandarin should be continued as "the primary language of instruction," while others were more emphatic in insisting that it be used exclusively "in all subjects, except foreign languages" for such varied reasons as "the propagation of Chinese virtues," "the enhancement of Chinese education in Singapore," or the "widespread understanding and the practical value of Chinese."

> Nantah is a Chinese university and it must not accept students who are incompetent in Chinese.--Commerce/2/M

> Mandarin should be the language of instruction for the Chinese university; therefore, it should recruit /as faculty/ only those who can speak Mandarin, except for the Language departments. I strongly object to English on the blackboards.-- Science/2/M

> Do not recruit lecturers who can't speak Mandarin for very few students are well versed in English.--Arts/2/M

Although the three outspoken statements just cited were all made by men students, it would appear from the statistical summary on this particular issue, that the women were on the whole significantly more ethnocentric than the men. It would also appear that, of the five major ethnic groups on the campus, the students of Hakka and Hainanese parentage were notably more disposed to favor the use of Chinese as the language of instruction at

252

Nanyang, while the students of Hokkien ancestry were least so disposed.[7] This is a further confirmation of the principle noted in chapter 5 that the ethnic groups with minimum prestige in the larger racial community are frequently most concerned about retaining the status and reputation of the more inclusive group.

Malay was, of course, the one language widely used in Southeast Asia which could be regarded as indigenous and therefore entitled, following national independence, to special consideration as the official medium of communication among the entire population. As noted earlier, the strongly anti-colonial sentiment at the close of the war and the movement to integrate Singapore politically within Malaysia led the heads of state to assume that Malay should be designated as the national language, not only in Malaya, but in Singapore as well, and this official preferential status has been nominally maintained ever since. During the height of the Independence struggle, the Singaporean of Chinese ancestry who subsequently became the first Prime Minister of the independent state, expressed the certainty that "the Malay language and the Malay culture will irresistibly become the predominant language and the predominant culture."[8] It would not seem, however, from the survey findings that

253

the generation of students at Nanyang at the end
of the 1960s shared that conception to any marked
degree. The fact that 71 percent of the students
disagreed, and 48 percent disagreed very strongly,
with the proposition that "Malay ought to be
Singapore's only national language," could, of
course, be interpreted as testimony of their
support to multilingualism--that other languages
such as Chinese or English might equally merit
such a designation. There was a relatively
significant minority of 13.1 percent, not all derived by any means from students in the small
department of Malay Studies, who indicated their
support of the designation, then in effect, of
Malay as the only national language.

Slightly over half of the students (54.2 percent), on the other hand, denied that proper
citizenship in Singapore was dependent on the ability to speak Malay, although nearly a quarter (24.2
percent) were in general agreement with that contention. It was also apparent that the students
from Malaya were more vocal about the desirability of the residents in both countries learning
to use Malay as their common medium of communication. Spontaneous statements by students to the
effect that "the Malay language is equally important in both countries; if both races are to

254

live in harmony," and that "learning each other's language and cultural traits is of great necessity," were by no means frequent, but they did occur, along with suggestions for increased library facilities and graduate studies in Malay language and culture, as well as for the admission of more Malay students. There were less pronounced variations among the five major ethnic groups or between the two sexes on the issue of the common use of the Malay language in Singapore than on the retention of Chinese as the dominant language of instruction at Nanyang. Although here also the women students were less liberally inclined than the men, that is, disposed to recognize the desirability of learning a different language. Unquestionably many of the same conceptions of their character and culture which contributed to the low rating of Malays as potential marriage mates (chapter 5)--their reputed lack of an ancient and honored cultural tradition and the resulting defects in conduct as viewed from Chinese perspective--lie back of the disposition to depreciate the Malay language as worthy of study by non-Malayans.

Student reactions to the desirability of English as a common medium of communication in Singapore reflects still another set of influences, such as the survival of colonial or anticolonial prejudices, or considerations of the use of English as an éntré to a world of scholarship, technology, and commercial interchange which are not available through other media. Despite the vigorous rejection of the English language, as symbolizing to leaders of the Independence movement, the survival of offensive colonial controls, nevertheless English has continued to be "the language of government, the courts, commerce and the University."[9] The purely utilitarian values of a command of the English language might therefore be widely recognized, even though its extensive use for ordinary purposes by the entire population or even as a basis of citizenship might be disputed.

Thus, nearly half of the Nanyang students (49.5 percent) took issue with the proposition that, "to be good citizens of Singapore, everyone should learn to speak English," while 29.4 percent professed to be in agreement with the idea. These findings indicate a greater preference on the part of Nanyang students for the community-wide use of English than of Malay, but it appears in this instance that the women are on the whole more favorably disposed than the men toward the widespread use of the additional language.

Insofar as the students spontaneously mentioned the use of a foreign language on the campus,

256

the sentiment was overwhelmingly, in a ratio of
three to one, in favor of increasing and strengthen-
ing the teaching and encouraging the use of English
both in courses and by students on the campus,
chiefly for its practical value. Typical written
comments of proposed changes at Nanyang by both
men and women in all three colleges urged that the
standards of English be raised "so that students
will find it easier when they go abroad for additional studies," "that more of the courses be
offered in the English language," "that compulsory
courses in English be set up with primary emphasis
on oral practice," and that "the students be encouraged to make a wider use of the English
language." Probably there is a dual concern which
underlies the reactions of a considerable number
of the students which is expressed in one comment,
"Preserve the Chinese character of Nantah, but at
the same time raise its English standard." On the
other hand, a small minority of students took the
initiative to express their desire that English be
abolished as a medium of instruction and that steps
be taken "to prevent Nantah from becoming an
English university."

The Goal of Racial Equality

Undoubtedly the distinguishing characteristic of
Singapore's multiracialism as differentiated from

257

that of Malaysia--a distinction which figured prominently in the separation of Singapore from Malaysia in 1965--was the central emphasis in the island metropolis of affording equal opportunity to all persons regardless of their racial affiliations or ancestry. Although the Federal Constitution of Malaysia provides that "all persons are equal before the law and entitled to the equal protection of the law. Except as expressly authorized by this Constitution, there shall be no discrimination against citizens on the ground of religion, race, descent or place of birth . . . " provision was made in article 153 "to safeguard the special position of the Malays . . . ."[10] This much debated clause, giving special privileges to Malays in public service, scholarships and educational facilities, and business permits and licences, has been rationalized as a means of counterbalancing the economic advantages which the immigrant groups had attained over the "indigenes," but it is nevertheless racially discriminatory.

Singapore's proposal for resolving the obvious economic imbalance between the rurally minded Malays and the aggressive and more successful urban dwellers of immigrant stocks was to restore the equilibrium through education and thereby establish a parity of opportunity among

258

all people, regardless of their racial or cultural antecedents. Special facilities with respect to education would be provided the Malays inasmuch as the laissez faire policy during the colonial period had permitted them to fall seriously behind the other immigrant groups in this regard, but in other aspects of the law it was assumed that a Malay would be treated no differently than persons of any other racial extraction. The principle of equal treatment across all racial or ethnic lines was less frequently explicitly stated in the official pronouncements and rhetoric than such terms as multiracialism or multilingualism; it was rather an attribute or condition assumed to be inherent in multiracialism and not needing to be specifically mentioned.

Three statements of a somewhat abstract nature, but referring quite clearly to the principle of equal treatment, were included in the Nanyang questionnaire in order to ascertain how the students stood on this fundamental issue. All three statements focus on the central concern for racial equality, but with the first centering on the cultural aspects while the other two mention specifically the economic (see Table 11). Although the majority of the students were in agreement with all three statements, there was far less opposition

259

Table 11

Agreement of Nanyang Students with Statements on Racial Equality (in percent)

Statement	Agree		No Opinion	Disagree	
	Strongly	On the Whole		On the Whole	Strongly
33. The future welfare of Singapore demands that the system of separate but equal cultural streams be continued indefinitely.	55.9	30.4	8.2	3.4	2.1
26. Singapore's future stability depends upon its ability to maintain an even balance in the economic status of its major ethnic groups.	25.5	38.2	14.7	15.1	6.5
38. There is no reason to believe that basic equality in economic achievement among the several racial groups in Singapore cannot be attained.	16.7	36.3	28.7	12.8	5.5

to item 33, the idea of cultural equality (5.5 percent), as contrasted with the 18.3 and 21.6 percent
opposition to the urgency or the feasibility of
economic equality across racial or ethnic lines. It
is significant also that the proportion of the students expressing agreement with all three or these
"officially correct" statements drops from the
strikingly high of 86.3 percent on the necessity of
cultural equality among the various groups to 63.7
percent on the desirability of economic equality and
still lower to 53.0 percent on the feasibility of
such equality. The only issue on which there was
any significant difference in the reactions of the
two sexes was item 26, on the desirability of
economic equality across ethnic lines, which was
opposed by 25.1 percent of the men, as compared
with only 17.6 percent of the women students, but
this is an area in which men would probably feel
the pinch of discrimination and competition more
keenly than women.

No specific encouragement was given the students to comment on any of these statements, but as
indicated earlier both men and women students from
Malaysia were frequently bitter in commenting on
the discrimination from which they allegedly
suffered in the competition for employment in that
country. And the sentiments expressed on the

question of interracial marriage (chapter 5) clearly indicate that much of the adverse feelings on the part of the women students toward all the non-Chinese groups, but especially toward the Malays, was derived from the conviction that the outgroups were less capable economically and therefore less deserving. Informal discussions in a class on race relations and with students on the campus revealed a common assumption that the Malays in particular had neither the inclination nor the capacities necessary for economic success in a modernized and competitive society. While conceding that the commonly recognized gap between the average per capita incomes of Malays and Chinese in both Singapore and Malaysia, despite the discriminatory legislation, was a major threat to the social stability of the region, and that theoretically it needed to be closed, there was still some reluctance to accept the alternative of rewarding people solely on the basis of race rather than on the basis of what they had rightfully earned.

Social Control and a Rugged Society

The deeply ingrained conviction in most peasant societies that "in the sweat of thy face shalt thou eat bread" has, of course, played a dominant role in the experience of the overseas Chinese in

262

both Singapore and other parts of Southeast Asia.
Terms such as industrious, frugal, thrifty, and en-
terprising appear repeatedly in the descriptions
of the Chinese in this part of the world, even
though an odious connotation has sometimes been
implied. Nurtured for many generations in an
economy of scarcity and compelled by circumstance
to work hard merely for survival in the new overseas setting, the Chinese immigrants do not need
to be persuaded of the merit of industry and the
application of effort, and these values were so
deeply implanted in the ethos of the people that
even the children and grandchildren, in a more
affluent setting, were likely to absorb them
emotionally almost along with their mother's milk.

The efforts of the government of Singapore,
especially after separation from Malaysia, to drive
home the necessity of a frugal, disciplined economy
could, therefore, be readily appreciated within the
Chinese community, and they simply reenforced
dispositions which were already there, at least
among the mass of the residents. Nevertheless,
repeated expressions from prominent figures in
government did keep such moral imperatives in the
forefront of public attention. The recurring theme
in the pronouncements by the Prime Minister and his
colleagues in government and carried widely through-

263

out the community by the mass media was upon the urgency of a realistic appraisal of the situation in which Singapore found itself after Separation and the readiness of its population to meet the new demands.

The moral tone, implied in the widely stressed goal of "the lean and rugged society," would have to be directed to the very practical ends of performing the tasks for which Singapore was best situated in the modern world. In one of many such public appeals "to create that mood in our people and be prepared to sacrifice, to make the effort to respond to a harsher situation," Lee Kuan Yew stated in May 1967:

> It is not just physical and psychological ruggedness alone which is required . . . . When we talk of leanness, it means that . . . every single person in Singapore now . . . must either pull his weight or he deserves what he will get. If we do not measure up to the challenge we deserve to perish either as individuals or as a community . . . . I take comfort from the fact that, after two years, our people are in a mood of grim determination, with a keenness to adjust ourselves to the new situation, to gird ourselves to make the grade. We will get what we can earn and earn what we strive for.[11]

The parallel emphasis upon the modernization of the economy--of obtaining preeminence in modern science and technology for the most effective functioning in the contemporary world--was equally

264

apparent in government pronouncements in the years following Separation.

Chinese temper and tradition would seem to give support to the governmental stress upon the necessity of a realistic approach to the problems of human survival--of accepting and adapting to the rigors of life, whatever they may be. It is not nearly so apparent that they are temperamentally disposed always to follow foreign models in meeting these problems, especially insofar as these patterns emanate from civilizations of recent origin and are therefore assumed to be immature and crude. Unquestionably the great majority of the Singapore residents who had been born and nurtured in China would accept Lin Yutang's contention that the Chinese way of life made them "lay emphasis on certain common virtues, like endurance, industry, thrift, moderation and pacifism . . . . We are an old nation. The eyes of old people see in its past and in this changing modern life much that is superficial and much that is of true meaning to our lives. We are a little cynical about progress."[12] Insofar as the Malaysian-born generations have shared in the values and dispositions of their China-born forebears, they too might entertain some doubts as to the necessary superiority of the science and technology from the West.

265

Table 12
Acceptance by Nanyang Students of Statements
on Modernization and the Rugged Society (in percent)

Statement	Agree		Neutral	Disagree	
	Strongly	On the Whole		On the Whole	Strongly
28. There is considerable danger that Singapore's future may be jeopardized by its taking over too much of the soft, permissive, and undisciplined ways of European and American society.	67.1	21.5	5.0	3.3	3.1
29. Modernization is the one objective to which all others must be subordinated if Singapore is to achieve its true destiny.	36.9	39.8	14.8	7.1	1.4
35. To have succeeded in placing one quarter of its population in public housing flats such as those at Queenstown is unquestionably one of Singapore's finest achievements for its people.	21.5	44.3	21.0	9.9	3.3

Table 12 (continued)

Statement	Agree		Neutral	Disagree	
	Strongly	On the Whole		On the Whole	Strongly
34. Increasing emphasis should be given to the University courses in the natural and physical sciences whose findings can be readily translated into the advancement of Singapore's industry and business.	13.5	32.1	15.2	24.5	14.7
30. In order to attain its one major objective of moderniza-tion, Singapore may have to resort to more drastic methods, including restrictions on freedom of speech and of assembly.	3.2	4.5	13.0	33.3	46.0

Some indication of the extent to which Nan-yang student opinion coincides with or diverges from the official formulations of policy on these dual aspects of what is expected of citizens of Singapore in the 1970s is reflected in their reactions to the five statements in Table 12.

Probably the most startling of the findings from Table 12 is the very high degree of consensus on items 28 and 30 among the students, one stressing the dangers of undue absorption of Western practices and the other emphasizing the possible necessity of employing drastic methods in attaining the objective of modernization. On no other item in the entire set of sixteen statements concerning contemporary life to which the students were asked to express an opinion was there such a high degree of unanimity of strong support or of strong disapproval as on item 28. (The high proportion of strong disapproval on item 30 is significant chiefly by way of contrast with the strong support on 28.) On this item, as on most of the others, the women were slightly more conservatively disposed than the men, with 91.7 percent of the women supporting the statement as compared with 87.1 percent of the men.

There are, of course, various ways of interpreting the expression of such strong concern on

268

the part of Nanyang students for the jeopardy Singapore might experience from the spread of undisciplined modes of conduct from the West. It would seem quite probable that a number of direct and unequivocal statements by high government officials attacking such influences and the forthright action by the Singapore police following the May 13th rioting in Malaysia must certainly have had some effect on student opinion. Less than two months prior to the survey, Lee Kuan Yew in a widely published address to the Association of Nanyang Graduates had warned that "Singaporeans bring in Western fads and fetishes at their own peril." Although presumably directed primarily toward "young English-stream students who have no grounding in their own cultural values and want to get 'with it,'" the message obviously applied to all.

> They want to imitate the activities
> and attitudes of the new left or
> SDS--Students for a Democratic
> Society. Whilst such student aber-
> rations will not wreck America or
> Western Europe, they will surely
> ruin Singapore . . . and in the
> interest of all, we cannot and will
> not allow this permissive, escapist,
> drug-taking, self indulgent promiscuous
> society to infect our young. Those who
> try to introduce such habits do so at
> their own peril, for we shall take im-
> mediate and anti-septic measures to
> prevent and scotch any such infection
> or affectation. The choice before us
> is constant vigilance or a complacent

slide to perdition.[13]

It was reported in the same source that Lee's warning was "the latest in a series of similar pronouncements by Government leaders" who "expressed concern over the behaviour of some students particularly a section in the University of Singapore."

It is quite probable also that this vigorous disavowal of European and American values by the students was at the same time a manifestation of ethnocentrism or at least of loyalty to the Singapore ways of life, as reflected earlier in this study. The almost unanimous disclaimer of the "soft" ways of the West could also be interpreted as an expression of an eagerness to engage in or at least a willingness to endure the "tough, resolute and highly disciplined community" which had been described as the destiny of Singapore during its early history.

Almost equally impressive, however, was the student endorsement of the trends in Singapore toward modernization, which had thus far largely consisted of the application of the science and technology so largely generated in the West. Although more than three-quarters of the students (76.7 percent) gave some sort of approval to the principle of modernization, it was not a strikingly enthusiastic endorsement, markedly less so

270

on the part of the women than of the men. Here
also, it is likely that the very strong support
which the state administration has given to industrial and commercial development and to applied
science and technology in education had registered
in the judgments of the students--more so in the
case of the men than of the women. The statement
on public housing, included in the survey as a
somewhat incidental test of student reactions to
governmental welfare programs, calls attention to
one of the most impressive forms of modernization
in Singapore, and the distribution of responses
by the students to that statement can also be
interpreted as an endorsement of this development,
albeit less enthusiastic than on the previous
proposition.

On two of the items in Table 12, the student
responses reflect definitely a critical point of
view toward policies of the administration, and
in this respect may give evidence of a more
wholesome independence of mind and spirit than in
any perfunctory or supine acceptance of authorita-
tive affirmations. There is, of course, no reason
to assume that the generous support which Nanyang
students gave to the ideas thus far presented in
this chapter were of such an uncritical nature, but
their reactions to items 30 and 34 in Table 12,

together with some of the written comments included elsewhere in the survey, clearly indicate the presence of a disposition toward independently open and rational judgments, essential for proper balance in a rapidly changing community.

There can be little doubt as to the propriety of the decision by the state administrators that the survival of Singapore as an independent nation depends largely on its ability to supply the technological and industrial skills of the sort especially needed in Southeast Asia and that the educational program by the state must be geared with these practical considerations in mind. Understandably, therefore, government officials, including the Prime Minister and members of his cabinet, had repeatedly emphasized the importance of competence in technology and applied science, and the 45.6 percent of Nanyang's students--principally drawn from the colleges of Science and Commerce--who registered agreement with statement 34 were undoubtedly similarly convinced and genuinely so. It is worth noting, however, that more than a third of the students (39.2 percent) expressed disagreement with the idea that increased emphasis was needed for the natural and physical sciences, this opposition coming most markedly in the College of Arts and from students of Hakka and Hainanese

272

ancestry.

It is, however, on the issue of freedom of speech and assembly that the independence of spirit among the Nanyang students becomes most apparent. The highest percentage of opposition and in its most intense form on any of the sixteen Singapore affairs statements was registered on proposition no. 30 in Table 12. Nearly half of the students indicated that they disagreed very strongly with this statement and a total of 79.3 percent indicated some degree of opposition, while only 7.7 percent agreed with the statement. It is unfortunate that the main thrust of this statement on freedom of speech and assembly was associated at all with modernization, but it seems unlikely that any significant number of the students were diverted by the dependent clause.

The restraints that an earlier administration felt necessary to impose on student organizations and activities of all sorts, in order to assure the government and the general public that communist influences were not in control, obviously rankled with the students in 1969. The virtual closing for some time of the Student Union building, the barbed wire fences around the women's dormitories and their early closing at night, and the presence on the campus of an external police force or "guards," all had been interpreted to some degree as a lack of confidence by the administration in the ability of the students to govern themselves and were correspondingly resented. This undoubtedly contributed substantially to the low rating by the students to another question regarding "the opportunities for free discussion," which was reported as satisfactory by only 14.0 percent of the respondents, despite the gradual relaxing of such restrictions by the new administration. The far larger proportion of the students (60.7 percent) designated this aspect of campus life as at least somewhat unsatisfactory, reenforcing their judgments by such comments as, "there has never been any encouragement for discussion," or "the opportunities for free discussion have been too limited." Scattered comments carried a decidedly cynical note: "Nantah is not a free university like some in the U.S. Karl Marx, Stalin, Lenin, and Mao are dangerous topics in discussion, according to the government," or "there is very little opportunity, for as the proverb goes, 'there are ears in the wall.'" On the other hand, in the listing by the students of proposed improvements on the campus, the providing of free discussion "any time, any place, with any person," as one student phrased it, had a high priority.

274

Concluding Observations

Probably the questions most likely to remain in the minds of the readers center upon the issue of multiracialism as affecting the future residents of Southeast Asia. Is it reasonable to expect that graduates of Nanyang, subjected as they have been to the massive influences in community and family settings so overwhelmingly Chinese, could or would incorporate, into their style of life, patterns of behavior consistent with the public professions of tolerance and equity toward the non-Chinese peoples of the region? How realistic, in terms of student participation and leadership, are the administrative designs for a smoothly functioning community consisting of such diverse cultural and linguistic strains? How imaginative and daring are the 1969 generation of Nanyang students likely to be in dealing with the problems of ethnic and racial relations which Singapore faces in the remaining decades of the twentieth century? Will Nanyang students pursue the highly individualistic and competitive goals that have played such a central part in their academic endeavors after graduation, goals which, in the wider community, have contributed so significantly to the economic disparities and tensions across racial lines? Will they accept without serious dissent or questioning

275

the definitions of civic relations which emanate
from the governments of either Singapore or the
Peoples Republic of China or from their own
ethnic group?

Although no fully conclusive answers to any of
these questions could be provided from this or any
other study, since the factors affecting the individuals involved or the group as a whole are too
many and diverse, additional light seems likely to
come from viewing the available data in total
perspective.

In view of the reputation, which the administration and the students of Nanyang acquired from
the time of the university's founding in 1953 and
sustained until the middle 1960s, as a generating
center for "Chinese communism and chauvinism," the
apparent calm on the Nanyang campus and the relative absence of student unrest at the close of the
1960s may seem difficult to comprehend. Why should
this former volcano of racialist subversion have
quite suddenly lost its fire? Had a new breed of
students with less aggressive dispositions and less
zeal for reform come into being, or were they
shrewdly holding their fire for a more strategic
occasion?

A distinct shift has occurred in the political
and economic atmosphere of both Singapore and

276

Malaysia following the 1965 Separation, and this has had its inevitable consequences within the Chinese communities of the entire region, as well as within the university designed primarily to serve these communities. The creation of a separate and independent nation of Singapore has enabled and, to a degree, required an even more forthright and explicit expression of its policy of multiracialism than had been possible or advisable within the Federation or as an integral part of Malaysia. Following separation, the governmental pronouncements insisting upon tolerant and equalitarian treatment across racial and ethnic lines have been so prominently expressed in official speeches and through the mass media as to become quite definitely implanted in the public consciousness, if not necessarily as firmly incorporated in the habits and practices of the people. The statement of the Prime Minister, quoted earlier in this chapter, affirming multiracialism as a central precept in the constitution of the new Republic of Singapore, has been paraphrased many times since by himself and by members of his cabinet and other prominent officials, and the impact has inevitably been felt at all levels of the educational system.

Data from the survey of Nanyang students indicate quite conclusively their readiness to concur intellectually in propositions of this type, but, of course, this does not mean that their conduct will wholly coincide. Indeed, it would be strange if there were no significant variance between the idealistic professions by the students within the confines of the academic setting and their actual practice in a workaday world much as there is between the rhetorical policy statements by top-ranking officials and the actual execution of these proposals by their subordinates. Certainly in the case of the students, the composite impact of the home, school, and a predominantly Chinese community setting is to confirm the conviction that no set of cultural traditions and goals could equal in value their own. Despite the humanistic "love of all men," which figures so prominently in Confucian doctrine and hence as a guiding principle of life for the followers of the Sage, it must be recognized that the natural pride of heritage among the Chinese leads them to preserve a proper social distance from those who fall short of such endowment. The Nanyang students, on the basis of their family and educational experience, seem to have absorbed a greater concern for the preservation of their ancestral integrity and purity than of the Confucian heritage with which it is supposedly so intimately related.

278

The evidence from this study and of casual observation on the Nanyang campus during 1969 reveals at the same time, however, a striking degree of tolerance toward the differing practices and traditions of people who are not Chinese. Although quite disdainful of the non-Chinese lifestyles for themselves, the Nanyang students manifest virtually no disposition to impose their own values upon others. Rather, a policy of "live and let live" seems to prevail, and it is unlikely, barring unforeseen contingencies, that this forbearing quality will diminish to any considerable degree as the present generation of students takes its place in the larger community of Southeast Asia. The fact that equanimity and calm were so well preserved on the Nanyang campus under the extreme provocation of the May rioting in Malaysia, in which the lives and property of relatives and fellow Chinese were so extensively threatened or destroyed, gives added grounds for thinking that this spirit of racial tolerance may continue under the stresses likely to develop in the future.

In the light of the excessive turmoil over the issue of communism on the Nanyang campus during the first few years of its existence, the relative absence of concern on this score in the late 1960s may seem equally paradoxical. Except for minimal

279

reference by students in the questionnaires to the relative absence of literature from the Peoples Republic in the library or to the hesitance about discussing such topics in classes or elsewhere on the campus, there was very little evidence that this was even a matter of interest to the students. It was scarcely mentioned as a topic of informal discussion among them.

Protest of any sort was clearly at a low ebb among the Nanyang students during 1969. Dissatisfaction on the part of individuals with various aspects of campus life, including the examination system, library facilities, housing, counseling, health and medical services, among others, was freely and vigorously expressed by the students through the questionnaire,[14] and to a limited degree by direct approach to the administration, but there was no overt rioting or evidence of the hostility and violence which was manifested during the 1950s and early 1960s. In contrast also with the belligerence and animosity shown by university students toward the established order in other parts of the world, notably in America and Europe but evident to some degree even in other institutions of higher learning in Southeast Asia, Nanyang students might have been characterized as placid or conformist on the basis of their external behavior.

280

Their uncensored reactions to national policy statements were so overwhelmingly favorable that, on the basis of this evidence alone, one might credit them with being government agents or puppets, but their equally vigorous insistence on the necessity of preserving freedom of speech and of assembly invalidates such an impression. While accepting willingly the government's stress upon a rugged and highly disciplined society, as being consistent with their own traditions, the Nanyang students by and large retained a basic independence of spirit which could lead them to resist with equal energy governmental constraints which came to be conceived as overly repressive.

The Nanyang students in the late 1960s gave evidence of being a more seasoned, disciplined, and possibly disillusioned generation than their predecessors at the university, a decade or so earlier. The Chinese community as a whole in both Singapore and Malaysia, and certainly the governmental administration of Singapore, had also attained in the preceding decade far greater political maturity, particularly in dealing with the problems of a multiracial society, and the students at the secondary and tertiary levels inevitably also acquired a more realistic outlook as a consequence. Foreign observers of liberal bents have expressed misgivings in the late 1960s lest the excessive concern by the Singapore administration for industrial advancement and efficiency and the demands of its rugged multiracial society might run afoul of either the deeply intrenched racial sensitivities,[15] on the one hand, or of the equally forceful demands for individual freedom of action, on the other hand.

Both of these potentially hazardous dispositions were operative to some degree among the students of Nanyang, but neither of them seemed strong enough to threaten the stability of either the state or the university. From my point of view, it would seem that despite the obvious potency and persistence of ethnic pride among the Nanyang students and its linkage during earlier years with the communist philosophy of the Peoples Republic, the probable menace to the political stability of the state from the part which Nanyang alumni might play in this area is relatively slight and is becoming progressively less.

Nanyang graduates of the early 1970s are not likely to advance with any noticeable rapidity either the biological fusion of the varied races of Southeast Asia or the cultural assimilation within the area, but neither are they likely to retard it below the pace implicit in the present administra-

tion's policy of multiracialism. Despite the overwhelming predominance of the Chinese in Singapore's population and even in the major cities of
Malaysia, the very nature of urban life inevitably
compels a considerable degree of at least surface
contact across ethnic and racial lines, which the
humane dispositions of Nanyang students may not
markedly hasten, but certainly will not delay.
Undoubtedly the philosophy of "live and let live"
inherent in multiracialism is the only realistic
and practicable policy to pursue under the conditions of life existing in Singapore, and Nanyang
students obviously recognize the wisdom of lending
it support.

There is somewhat greater probability that
Nanyang graduates of the 1970s will react nega-
tively to what is interpreted as excessive pressure
either from the university or the state to restrict
or channel their thinking or discussion of new or
foreign ideas. Despite the insistence of Lee Kuan
Yew and his close governmental colleagues on pro-
tecting Singapore's youth from the soft, indulgent
ways of the West and its vagrant ideas, there does
not seem to be any effective means of placing a
permanent embargo on such intrusive influences. In
a community with as deeply rooted a tradition of
free trade as Singapore the likelihood of success

283

in preventing the free flow of ideas appears remote. Attempts to stifle such trade among persons with as much pride as the students of Nanyang may simply precipitate greater determination to secure access to such forbidden fruit. On the other hand, the evidence of this study and especially of this chapter reveals a decided disposition among these students to give intellectual support to the crucial policies of the government on multiracialism and racial equality and to accept such demands of frugality, discipline, and even of regimentation as might be necessary to bring about their achievement. Their professions, of course, can only be validated by their performances under the stress of crisis situations as they may arise, but the restraint and outward calm maintained by the students themselves under the extreme provocations of the May 13th incidents augurs well for their rationally controlled conduct in the future. One could wish that similar restraint and rationality were exercised in the formulation and execution of policies respecting race relations by the governments with which the Nanyang students will be involved in the future.

Notes

1. James W. Gould, The United States and Malaysia (Cambridge, Massachusetts, 1969), p. 131.

2. Alex Josey, Lee Kuan Yew (Singapore, 1968), pp. 435-436.

3. Ibid., p. 141.

4. Ibid., p. 143.

5. Ibid., p. 521.

6. Rayson L. Huang, "A Talk to the Rotary Club," The Bulletin of Nanyang University, I, 22 (Sept., 1969), p. 18.

7. The proportions of the students indicating that they favored instruction primarily in the Chinese language were as follows in the several ethnic groups: Hokkiens, 78.5 percent; Cantonese, 80.0 percent; Teochews, 82.4 percent; Hakka, 83.7 percent; and Hainanese, 84.6 percent. Among the men students as a whole, the proportion so disposed was 78.4 percent, as compared to 84.5 percent among the women students.

8. Quoted in Josey, op. cit., p. 66.

9. Josey, ibid., p. 65.

10. Malaysia Federal Constitution (Kuala Lumpur, 1968) articles 8 and 153.

11. Josey, op. cit., pp. 552-553.

12. Lin Yutang, My Country and My People (New York, 1935), pp. 346-347.

13. Straits Times, 21 August 1969, p. 1.

14. Elaborated in the confidential report to the administrative staff of Nanyang University on part 3 of the questionnaire.

15. See, for example, the statement by Derek Davies, "Rugged Sensitivity," Far Eastern Economic Review, 21 August 1969, p. 461.

APPENDIX

A RACIAL INDEX OF OCCUPATIONAL STATUS

One simple and useful indication of the state of
race relations in any community is the degree of
representation of its several ethnic groups in
different types of occupations. If the persons
providing the economic support for the households
of a particular racial or ethnic group are wholly
or largely confined to occupations which are poorly
paid and are involved in socially distasteful
tasks, this reflects the low position commonly
accorded to members of this group in the larger
community. The impact of such occupational segregation becomes all the more meaningful when it is
known or widely believed that other racial groups
in the same community have virtual control of the
more remunerative and desirable fields of employment. Members of racial groups in this latter
category obviously enjoy a higher rating and are
in a position to exercise greater power in the
community than the groups less fortunately situated.

Thus, the fact that all, or even a very high
percentage of all the heads of banking institutions
in a particular country were members of racial
groups A and B, while a similarly high proportion

of the ordinary laborers were members of groups C and D, would certainly give some indication of the relative status of these four groups. On the other hand, however, unless some account were also taken of the total number of persons in the entire population engaged in all forms of economically remunerative pursuits, such simple percentages could be quite misleading. For example, the 1957 Census of Population in Singapore reported that persons of Chinese ancestry constituted just 40 percent of all employees of the central, state, and local governments (not classified elsewhere), whereas only 25 percent of such employees were of the Malay race, and from this it might appear that the Malays were being discriminated against in favor of the Chinese. When it is recognized, however, that the Chinese made up more than 70 percent of the entire labor force of Singapore as against only 13 percent from among the Malays, it becomes clear that the Chinese were markedly underrepresented in proportion to their total employed population and the Malays were greatly overrepresented.

The index of occupational status is a simple device to compare the actual representation of each racial group engaged in specific occupations with that group's proportional representation in the entire labor force. It can be expressed as follows:

288

$$\text{Index of Occupational Status} = \frac{A_x}{T_t} \div \frac{A_t}{T_t}$$

where A_x is the number of persons in Group A engaged in any specific occupation, T_x is the total number from all groups engaged in that occupation, A_t is the total number from Group A in the entire labor force, and T_t is the total number from all groups in the entire labor force. Thus any index of less than unity indicates that the designated group is underrepresented in that particular occupation, while an index exceeding unity indicates that it is overrepresented.

SELECTED BIBLIOGRAPHY

Arasaratnam, Sinnappah, Indians in Malaysia and Singapore (Bombay, 1970)

Buckley, Charles Burton, An Anecdotal History of Old Time in Singapore (Kuala Lumpur, 1965)

Elegant, Robert S., The Dragon's Seed: Peking and the Overseas Chinese (New York, 1967)

Freedman, Maurice, and Willmott, William E., "Southeast Asia, with Special Reference to the Chinese," in UNESCO, Research on Racial Relations (Paris, 1966)

Ginsburg, Norton, and Roberts, Chester Fr., Jr., Malaya (Seattle, 1958)

Gould, James W., The United States and Malaysia (Cambridge, Massachusetts, 1969)

Gullick, J. M., Malaysia (New York, 1969)

Hunter, Guy, Southeast Asia: Race, Culture, and Nation (London, 1966)

Josey, Alex, Lee Kuan Yew (Singapore, 1968)

McKie, Ronald, The Emergence of Malaysia (New York, 1963)

Makepeace, Walter (editor), One Hundred Years of Singapore (London, 1921)

Miller, Harry, The Story of Malaysia (London, 1965)

Moore, Donald, and Moore, Joanna, The First 150 Years of Singapore (Singapore, 1968)

Ooi, Jin-Bee, and Chiang, Hai Ding (editors), Modern Singapore (Singapore, 1969)

Purcell, Victor, The Chinese in Malaya (London, 1967)

Rahman, Tun Abdul, May 13: Before and After (Kuala Lumpur, 1969)

Razak, Tun Abdul, The May 13 Tragedy: A Report of
    the National Operations Council (Kuala Lumpur,
    1969

Silcock, T. H., "The Effects of Industralization
    in Malaya," in Guy Hunter (editor), Indus-
    trialization and Race Relations (London, 1965)

Song Ong Siang, One Hundred Years' History of the
    Chinese in Singapore (Singapore, 1967)

Thomson, George C., Singapore: The Way Ahead
    (Singapore, 1967)

Tregonning, K. G., Malaysia and Singapore (Singa-
    pore, 1967

Van der Kroef, Justus M., Communism in Malaysia and
    Singapore (The Hague, 1967)

Winstedt, Sir Richard, The Malays: A Cultural
    History (London, 1961)

Official Reports

Singapore Year Book 1967 (Singapore, 1968)

Census Reports:

   Vlieland, C. A., A Report on the 1931 Census,
      British Malaya (London, 1932)

   Del Tufo, M. V., Malaya: A Report on the 1947
      Census of Population (London, 1949)

   Chua, S. C., Report on the Census of Popula-
      tion, State of Singapore (Singapore, 1964)

   Singapore Sample Household Survey, 1966,
      Report No. 1 (Singapore, 1967)

Government White Paper, Communism in the Nanyang
    University (Kuala Lumpur, 1964)

Wang Gungwu and others, Report of the Nanyang
    University Curriculum Review Committee
    (Singapore, 1965)

Nanyang University Calendar, 1969-1970 (Singapore,
    1969)

292

PREVIOUSLY PUBLISHED

(No. 1)   Bibliography of English Language Sources
          on Human Ecology, Eastern Malaysia and
          Brunei. Compiled by Conrad P. Cotter with
          the assistance of Shiro Saito. September
          1965. Two parts. Out of print.

(No. 2)   Economic Factors in Southeast Asian
          Social Change. May 1968. Robert Van
          Niel, editor. Out of print.

No. 3   East Asian Occasional Papers (1). Harry
          J. Lamley, editor. May 1969.

No. 4   East Asian Occasional Papers (2). Harry
          J. Lamley, editor. July 1970.

No. 5   A Survey of Historical Source Materials
          in Java and Manila. Robert Van Niel.
          February 1971.

(No. 6)   Educational Theory in the People's
          Republic of China: The Report of Ch'ien
          Chung-Jui. Translation by John N.
          Hawkins. May 1971. Out of print.

No. 7   Hai Jui Dismissed from Office. Wu Han.
          Translation by C. C. Huang. June 1972.

No. 8   Aspects of Vietnamese History. Edited
          by Walter F. Vella. March 1973.

No. 9   Southeast Asian Literature in Trans-
          lation: A Preliminary Bibliography.
          Philip N. Jenner. March 1973.

No. 10   Textiles of the Indonesian Archipelago.
          Garrett and Bronwen Solyom. October 1973.

No. 11   British Policy and the Nationalist Move-
          ment in Burma, 1917-1937. Albert D.
          Moscotti. February 1974.

No. 12   Aspects of Bengali History and Society.
          Edited by Rachel Van M. Baumer. In press.